OSCAR WILDE

VYVYAN HOLLAND

OSCAR WILDE

with 146 illustrations

THAMES AND HUDSON

To my dear friend REBECCA WEST

© 1960 Vyvyan Holland & Thames and Hudson Ltd, London

*Revised edition 1966
First paperback edition 1988
Reprinted 1997*

ISBN 0–500–26031–1

Printed and bound in Spain

Dublin in the eighteenth century; Oscar Wilde's ancestor, Colonel de Wilde, came to Ireland and founded the family in the seventeenth century

ON 16TH OCTOBER 1854, IN DUBLIN, was born one of the most remarkable and controversial figures in the history of English literature or, indeed, of the literature of the world: Oscar Wilde. His career may, without exaggeration, be described as kaleidoscopic and at the same time catastrophic; for never has any author's reputation passed through so many different phases—from ridicule to adulation, from adulation to fame, from triumphant fame to contempt, disgrace, and disdain, eventually to return, posthumously, to honour and triumph.

Wilde had the misfortune, or perhaps the fortune, to have been born and to have lived in the stiff-necked, prejudiced, and etiquette-ridden years of the Late Victorian Age. English Society was encompassed by conventionality: every utterance and every action of the individual were required to conform to rigid rules of behaviour and ethics, the slightest deviation from which being regarded as an outrage and as putting the offender 'beyond the pale'. Even the canons of art and literature were laid down and had to be adhered to. It was this state of affairs that Wilde made it his mission in life to break down, and it is a remarkable tribute to the forcefulness of his character that he largely succeeded in doing so, against overwhelming odds, and in making a position for himself in literature and Society that has seldom been equalled. So that his fall from grace was

William Wilde, Oscar's father,
as a young man of twenty-eight,
by Bernard Mulrenin, RHA

from so great a height that even the literary world of the period could not reassemble the fragments into which his reputation as a writer was shattered, and it was not until nearly twenty years after his death that his genius became once more universally recognised.

Wilde's family   A great deal of Wilde's character was directly attributable to his origin, and his career cannot be properly appraised without a brief outline of his ancestry. The family of Wilde was Dutch in origin; the name de Wilde is not an uncommon one in Holland today. All Oscar's biographers, following the lead of the first of them, Robert Sherard, put forward the story that the first Irish Wilde was a builder who migrated to Dublin from Wolsingham, a small town some twelve miles east of Durham. There is no foundation whatever for this. The name (pronounced 'de Vilde') became confused in the minds of the Irish country folk with 'the builder'; and the Wolsingham story was a figment of Sherard's imagination, he having somehow discovered that there were a number of people in that town bearing the name of Wilde. In point of fact, the first Wilde to settle in Ireland was a certain Colonel de Wilde, son of a Dutch painter, examples of whose work are to be seen in the Hague Art Gallery today. This Colonel de Wilde was a soldier of fortune who fought for King William III of England and was granted lands in Ireland by that monarch at the end of

A famous oculist and an
eminent physician—
Sir William Wilde and
Sir William Stokes

the seventeenth century. The Colonel married an Irish girl, settled down with her on his estates and, as is the way with settlers in Ireland, became more Irish than the Irish themselves. His property was in Connaught, and in due course one of his sons, Ralph, became agent to Lord Sandford, at Castlereagh in County Roscommon.

Ralph Wilde married a Miss Margaret O'Flynn, of Caher in County Galway, by whom he had three sons, one of whom, Thomas, was Oscar Wilde's grandfather. Thomas decame a doctor, and married a Miss Emily Fynne, daughter of John Fynne of Ballymagibbon in County Mayo, who was connected with some of the most important families in Connaught, among whom were the Surridges and the Ouseleys. He lived to a great age and practised medicine all round Castlereagh to the end of his life. He was a picturesque character and did all his rounds on horseback. As Mr T. G. Wilson, an eminent Irish surgeon, wrote of him: 'He must have been worth seeing, when at nearly eighty years of age he cantered along on his spanking chestnut, encased in his voluminous, many-caped riding-coat, broad-brimmed leather hat, buckskin smalls, top-boots, overalls and spatterdashes, with a red culgee coming up to the middle of his nose.'

Dr Thomas Wilde had three sons. The two elder became Church of England clergymen; the youngest, born in Castlereagh in 1815, was William Robert

Sir William Wilde at the
height of his fame

Wills Wilde, later to become Sir William Wilde and Oscar Wilde's father.
Sir William was also a doctor, and became one of the most important aural
surgeons and oculists of his day; while still under forty he was appointed
Surgeon-Oculist to Queen Victoria. He has been called 'the father of modern
otology'. He was also an eminent archaeologist and wrote about a dozen books
on Irish folk-lore, legend, and tradition.

Oscar's mother   William Wilde married a famous Irishwoman, Jane Francesca Elgee, the
daughter of a Wexford lawyer. She was born in 1826, and, while still in her
teens, became an ardent Irish patriot, embracing the cause of the Irish against
what they called their English oppressors with all the enthusiasm and abandon
of a fiery nature. She wrote inflammatory political articles and poems, under the
name of John Fernshaw Ellis, and later under the name of Speranza. On more
than one occasion she was on the brink of being arrested and charged with high
treason. These activities culminated in 1848, with the publication of an article,

Jane Francesca Wilde
(*née* Elgee), Oscar's mother,
at the age of thirty-eight,
by Bernard Mulrenin, RHA

some six thousand words in length, entitled *Jacta est Alea* ('The Die is Cast'). Charles Gavan Duffy, the editor of the paper in which the article appeared, had been arrested some time before on charges of sedition, and at his trial the prosecuting counsel quoted passages from the article, against him, though he could not possibly have been responsible for it. Miss Elgee, who was in court, immediately rose to her feet and cried, with disdainful indifference: 'I am the criminal who, as author of the article, should be in the dock. I am the culprit, if culprit indeed there be!'

After her marriage Speranza's political enthusiasms and activities waned, and she settled down to domestic life and to writing poetry and books on Irish folklore, of which she made an exhaustive study; she also became the centre of a literary and artistic coterie in Dublin. The Wildes had three children, two boys and a girl. The eldest, William Wills Wilde, was born in 1853; he and Oscar went to school and to the University together and later he was called to the Irish

His brother and sister

9

Oscar Wilde in a blue velvet dress,
aged about two

Oscar's birth

Bar but soon tired of that life, became a journalist and was a well-known figure in Fleet Street, London, until his death in 1896. A year later, in 1854, the second son, Oscar, was born. His birth was somewhat of a disappointment to Speranza who all through her pregnancy had been quite certain the child was going to be the girl she longed for. And it is worthy of note that in those days when boys were dressed in skirts long after they could walk, she kept the child in such clothes until the beginning of her third pregnancy in 1857. There has recently come to light a coloured photograph or Daguerreotype of Oscar in a blue velvet dress, aged about two.

Oscar Wilde was born at No. 21, Westland Row, Dublin, the house from which Dr Wilde was carrying on his practice at the time. He was given the names Oscar Fingal O'Flahertie Wills. His mother's hand can clearly be seen in this. The name Oscar is that of the son of Ossian, the third-century Irish warrior bard; that earlier Oscar was killed at the battle of Gabhra, in single combat with King Cairbre; but the name was also that of the then reigning King of Sweden, who became Oscar's godfather after Dr Wilde had performed a successful operation on the King for cataract.

21, Westland Row, Dublin, where Oscar was born. The words in Erse on the plaque mean 'was born in this house'

Fingal was Ossian's father. Fingal was also the hero, in Ossian's poems, who delivered Erin from her enemies; perhaps Speranza saw herself as a reincarnation of him. The O'Flahertie no doubt came from some supposed or real connection with 'the ferocious O'Flaherties of Galway'. Wills was a family name of the Wildes. Oscar abandoned the last three names after leaving Oxford.

Isola Wilde

Two years after Oscar's birth, Mrs Wilde's dearest wish was fulfilled by the arrival of a daughter. She was christened Isola Francesca and from the day of her birth she was idolised by the whole family. She died after a short illness at the age of ten. This deeply affected Oscar; after his death an envelope was found in his possession on which was written:

> My Isola's Hair
> Obiit Feb XXIII
> 1867.
> She is not dead but sleepeth.

Many years later he wrote the poem *Requiescat* in her memory. In delicacy of feeling and in sadness without bitterness this poem has seldom been surpassed:

> *Tread lightly, she is near*
> *Under the snow,*
> *Speak gently, she can hear*
> *The daisies grow.*
>
> *All her bright golden hair*
> *Tarnished with rust,*
> *She that was young and fair*
> *Fallen to dust.*
>
> *Lily-like, white as snow,*
> *She hardly knew*
> *She was a woman, so*
> *Sweetly she grew.*
>
> *Coffin-board, heavy stone*
> *Lie on her breast,*
> *I vex my heart alone,*
> *She is at rest.*
>
> *Peace, Peace, she cannot hear*
> *Lyre or sonnet,*
> *All my life's buried here,*
> *Heap earth upon it.*

1, Merrion Square, Dublin, where most of Oscar's childhood was spent, and where Lady Wilde held her *salon*

The envelope decorated by Oscar when he was twelve years old to contain a lock of his sister's hair, which he kept until he died

Lough Corrib, in which lurked the 'great melancholy carp', and on the banks of which stood Moytura, Sir William Wilde's country house

Unfortunately, no portrait of Isola Wilde exists; or at least none that can be identified. The earliest portraits of the Wildes are indeed one of Dr William Wilde, by Bernard Mulrenin, RHA, at the age of twenty-eight, and one of Speranza, also by Mulrenin, at the age of thirty-eight. Both portraits were exhibited in the Royal Hibernian Academy in the years in which they were painted.

Early childhood Shortly after Oscar's birth, the family moved to an imposing mansion at 1, Merrion Square, Dublin, from which Dr Wilde continued to conduct his medical practice and where Mrs Wilde held her *salon* frequented by all the artists, writers, wits, intellectuals and, of course, the medical profession of the city. We know nothing of the early childhood of the Wilde children; so we must presume that it was an uneventful childhood, without any major crises except, of course, the death of Isola. An old proverb says, 'Happy is the country that has no history', and the same may be applied to children. William, Oscar, and Isola spent a good deal of their time at Moytura, Dr William's house on the shores of Lough Corrib, and in later life Oscar used to describe the 'great melancholy carp' which swam close in to the shore on the look-out for tit-bits from the children, too lazy to be frightened of them.

At school When Oscar Wilde was ten years old and his brother twelve, they were both sent to Portora Royal School, at Enniskillen. In spite of the difference in their ages, the boys seem to have been in the same class. Whereas Willie Wilde was

An engraving of Cong River and Ashford which is among the illustrations in *Lough Corrib* by Sir William Wilde

popular at school, Oscar was quite the reverse; he had little in common with the other boys, as he disliked games and fighting and took more interest in flowers and sunsets than he did in the possession of knives and other objects treasured by most small boys. And he seemed to have preferred his own company to that of his school-fellows, a preference which they seem to have reciprocated. He heartily disliked mathematics and anything to do with science. Indeed, his opinion of such scholastic attainments is well summed up in his own aphorism: 'Nothing that is worth knowing can be taught.' When he was bored with the subject of a lesson, he would try to lead the master into a digression by ingeniously worded questions which had nothing to do with the matter in hand. His main interests in scholarship were poetry and the classics, particularly Greek, for which he had an inordinate passion.

In October 1871, when he was just seventeen, he won an entrance scholarship to Trinity College, Dublin, which is the Protestant University of Ireland. There he remained for three years, and it was there that he fell under the spell of the Reverend John Pentland Mahaffy, Junior Fellow, Junior Dean, and Professor of Ancient History at the College. At the time, Professor Mahaffy was still in his early thirties; in those days it was extraordinary for anyone so young to hold such an exalted position; he was fascinated by Greek culture and exercised a very considerable influence on Oscar's later life.

Trinity College, Dublin

Trinity College, Dublin, in an eighteenth-century print; it remains unchanged today

At Trinity, Oscar shared rooms with his elder brother Willie. They lived in the quadrangle known, for some obscure reason, as 'Botany Bay', their rooms being on the first floor of No. 18. All the rooms in this building were the same, each having two bedrooms, a sitting-room, and a kind of pantry-larder.

Edward Carson

It was here that the life-long rivalry between Oscar Wilde and Edward Carson started. Wilde and Carson were exact contemporaries, but whereas Carson was forceful and industrious, Wilde was merely quick of wit and superficially brilliant. In 1873, Wilde obtained the greatest scholastic distinction open to a Trinity undergraduate, namely a Foundation Scholarship in classics. This entitled its holder to an annual income of £20 (in those days, but greatly increased since) for several years, to free rooms, and to many other privileges. Then, in 1874, he won the Berkeley Gold Medal for Greek, the highest classical award obtainable at the College, with a thesis on *The Fragments of the Greek Comic Poets, as Edited by Meineke*.

Carson also worked for a scholarship, but failed to reach the required standard. Oscar was well aware of the qualities, such as they were, that Carson possessed. Walking one day through the College with a friend, he said: 'There goes a man destined to reach the very top of affairs.' 'Yes,' replied his companion, 'and one who will not hesitate to trample on his friends in getting there.' This proved to be tragically prophetic so far as Wilde himself was concerned.

Rev. John Mahaffy

As already mentioned, Mahaffy was the greatest influence on Oscar Wilde's life at this period. In later years Wilde said:

The Rev. Sir John Pentland Mahaffy

The Berkeley Gold Medal for
Greek, won by Wilde in 1874

'I got my love of the Greek ideal and my intimate knowledge of the language
from Mahaffy and Tyrell. They were Trinity to me; Mahaffy was especially
valuable to me at that time. Though not so good a scholar as Tyrell, he had been
in Greece, had lived there and had saturated himself with Greek thought and
Greek feeling. Besides, he deliberately took the artistic standpoint towards everything, which was coming more and more to be my standpoint. He was a
delightful talker, too; a really good talker in a certain way—an artist in eloquent
words and vivid pauses.'

Oscar Wilde undoubtedly learned a great deal of the art of conversation from
Mahaffy. It is a sad reflection, then, that when the downfall came and someone
asked Mahaffy something about Oscar, Mahaffy replied: 'We no longer speak
of Mr Oscar Wilde.'

Whereas Oscar had been unpopular at school, he was universally liked at
Trinity. The verdict of one of his contemporaries was that 'he was a very good-
natured man and extraordinarily amusing'. He was beginning to find his feet.

He concluded his brilliant career at Trinity, Dublin, by winning a scholarship worth £95 a year, to Magdalen College, Oxford, and in October 1874,
when he was exactly twenty, he went up to the University.

It was at Oxford that the seeds of aestheticism and of the ideals of Greek
beauty that had been sown in Dublin by Mahaffy began to spring up and flower.
Oxford made an immediate impression on him, and it was not long before he

At Oxford

Magdalen College with its tower; one of the most beautiful of the Oxford Colleges

began to make an impression on Oxford. He was more than a year older than most of the other freshmen, and we have an excellent description of him from the pen of David Hunter Blair, written many years after Wilde's death, when he had become the Right Reverend Sir David Hunter Blair, Bart, OSB, Abbot of Dunfermline, who was in his second year when Oscar Wilde matriculated. He writes:

'I have a vivid recollection of him at our first meeting: the large features lit up by intelligence, sparkling eyes, and broad cheerful smile; altogether an attractive personality, enhanced by his extraordinary conversational abilities. One could not know him, even slightly, without realising that he had brilliant gifts, inherited from a father of exceptional mental powers, and a mother not less remarkable in a quite different way.'

Sir David pays a further tribute to Oscar's conversational powers. He describes the Sunday evening parties held in Oscar's rooms:

Cardinal Newman as a young man. Wilde referred to him as 'that divine man'

John Ruskin as a young man. He also exerted great influence over Wilde

'When the punch had been drunk, the lights extinguished, the piano closed, and the merry guests dispersed, there followed an hour or two which still, after sixty long years, linger vividly in my memory. Round the fire gathered Wilde, William Ward and I; just we three, and talked and talked as boys will—we were hardly more—*de omnibus rebus et quibusdem aliis,* as the old Roman jest was: about everything and other things as well. Oscar was always the protagonist in these midnight conversations, pouring out a flood of paradoxes, untenable propositions, quaint comments on men and things; and sometimes, like Silas Wegg, "dropping into poetry", spouting yards of verse, either his own or that of other poets whom he favoured. We listened and applauded and protested against some of his preposterous theories. Our talk was quite unrestrained and ranged over a vast variety of topics. Wilde said not a few foolish and extravagant things; but Ward and I could both testify, and it pleases me to emphasise this, that never, in our long and intimate intercourse, did we hear a coarse or unseemly word fall from his lips.'

Walter Pater.
Wilde fell under the spell of his
hedonistic teaching at Oxford

More than twenty years later, Wilde wrote that the two great turning-points in his life were when his father sent him to Oxford and when Society sent him to prison. Perhaps he said this in the spirit of paradox which never deserted him even during the closing years of his life. However, the seeds of aestheticism and of Hellenism that had been sown in his mind by Mahaffy would no doubt have sprung up in any case, though probably in a different form.

Ruskin

Three weeks after Oscar arrived at Magdalen he met John Ruskin, Slade Professor of Art at Oxford University, who had already acquired a European-wide reputation as an expert in art, architecture, and the history of the Renaissance in Italy. He had just started a course of lectures described as 'The Aesthetic and Mathematical Schools of Florence'. The first part of this title naturally appealed strongly to Wilde, who immediately enrolled himself as one of Ruskin's pupils. And as Ruskin proclaimed the necessity of beauty, the dignity of labour, and the ugliness of machinery, in a very short time Wilde became one of his most devoted followers.

Walter Pater

Although his first inspiration at Oxford was this contact with Ruskin, he afterwards became a disciple and follower of Walter Pater, who has been described by his admirers as the greatest influence of the century for the study and realisation of pure beauty, and by his enemies as the most baneful influence from which Oxford ever suffered.

Aestheticism

Oscar Wilde, already flamboyant in his dress and rapidly improving the art of conversation which he had studied and absorbed under the teaching of Mahaffy, found himself completely dominated by this obscure Fellow and Tutor

A group of Wilde's Oxford undergraduate friends

Oscar Wilde (*on the right*) in cricketing clothes

A group of dons and undergraduates with their relatives at Magdalen. Wilde is third from the left standing

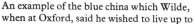
An example of the blue china which Wilde, when at Oxford, said he wished to live up to

Wilde's rooms in Magdalen from across the Cherwell

of Brasenose College, singularly unprepossessing in appearance, shy and retiring, yet utterly absorbed by theories of his own on the conduct of life. His doctrine was an exaltation of personal experience above all restrictions, as the object of life. 'The theory,' he wrote, 'or system which requires of us the sacrifice of any part of this experience, in consideration of some interest into which we cannot enter, or some abstract morality with which we have not identified ourselves, or what is only conventional, has no real claim on us.' And Pater declared that the ultimate wisdom consists in expanding our lives by 'getting as many pulsations as possible into a given time', together with 'the desire for beauty, the love of art for art's sake'. In other words, he preached that physical sensation is an end in itself, to which it is noble to aspire. Dangerous teaching for anyone as impressionable as Wilde, who promptly took up the cry of 'Art for Art's sake' as his slogan and the basis of his philosophy.

At the same time, as can be gathered from his letters, he felt strongly drawn towards the Roman Catholic Church, in which he was naturally encouraged

More college friends at Oxford

Dante's tomb at Ravenna

by Hunter Blair; and it is probable that he would have joined that Church, had it not been that he was afraid that in doing so he would bitterly wound the feelings of his family. He was especially attracted by the personality and the utterances of Cardinal Newman; in one of his letters he writes: 'I am going to see Newman at Birmingham, to burn my fingers a little more . . . I am awfully keen for an interview, not of course to argue, but merely to be in the presence of that divine man. I will send you a long account of it: but perhaps my courage will fail, as I could hardly resist Newman, I am afraid.'

This letter was written to one of his greatest friends at Oxford, William Walsford Ward, a year senior to himself at Magdalen, who became a distinguished lawyer in the West Country and was for some years Treasurer of the Society of Merchant Adventurers. They corresponded regularly during vacation time; Ward kept all Wilde's letters, which are now in the possession and keeping of Magdalen. They throw a great deal of light on Wilde's life at Oxford and in the vacations at that time. They show him to have lived a very normal undergraduate life, working fairly hard spasmodically in term time, playing games, giving and attending parties. In the vacations he would usually either go home to Ireland or to his uncle, the Reverend John Maxwell Wilde, who was the incumbent at West Ashby, a village some two miles north of Horncastle in

The ruins of the Roman Forum, photographed about the time of Wilde's visit

Lincolnshire. In Ireland he would spend his time riding, fishing, and shooting. At West Ashby he would play lawn tennis, a game then in its infancy, drink his uncle's good wine, and flirt with his pretty cousins. There is also in existence a diary kept by Ward's sister during 'Commem.' in 1876, in which Oscar frequently appears; the main interest of this diary is that it shows that, in spite of what one's elders may say, undergraduates in those days behaved just as badly as they do today, if not worse.

Italy

In the summer of 1875, Oscar Wilde made an extensive tour of northern Italy, visiting Genoa, Milan, Turin, Florence, Verona, Padua, Venice, Ravenna and ending up in Rome. It is to this visit that is owed the earliest known of Wilde's poems; it was the first of what was intended to be a series of poems on Italy and was entitled *Graffiti d'Italia: I. San Miniato;* only one other poem appeared in this series, namely *II, Arona. Lago Maggiore.* Even the first poem did not appear in print until much later. Indeed, the earliest actual work of Wilde's was the *Chorus of Cloud Maidens,* adapted from *The Clouds* of Aristophanes, which appeared in the *Dublin University Magazine* in November 1875. This Italian tour made a great impression on him and also increased his interest in the Roman Catholic Church, by putting him into such close touch with so many exquisite buildings and works of art that had been inspired by it.

A photograph of Oscar Wilde wearing Greek costume, taken in Athens

Oscar Wilde (*seated*) in fancy dress. As these photographs show he already delighted in dressing up

Greece

But a more important expedition took place in 1877, when Wilde and two other young men accompanied Professor Mahaffy on a tour of Greece. He was enchanted by everything he saw there. Even Athens was more wonderful than the idealised picture he had formed of it in his imagination, and he became more than ever absorbed in the Greek ideals of beauty. So absorbed, indeed, were the travellers that they overstayed their leave for a month; so that when Wilde returned to Oxford he was fined £45 by the College authorities; and even Mahaffy, eminent figure though he was at Trinity—got hauled over the coals.

Success at Oxford

In spite of continually complaining in his letters that he was idling and wasting his time, he must really have done a considerable amount of work, because in 1876 he took a first class in Moderations and in 1878 a first class in the Honour Finals, or 'Greats', as they are called, thus achieving the ambition of every classical student at Oxford, namely getting a 'Double First'. The Magdalen authorities were so pleased (and I think a little surprised) at this that they returned him the £45 they had fined him for his absence in Greece the year before.

In 1876 Wilde began seriously to write poetry and in this and the two following years he had a number of poems published, mostly in Oxford and in Irish

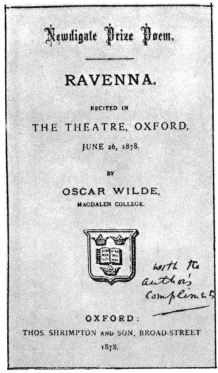

Wilde at the time of writing the Newdigate Prize Poem

The cover of the prize-winning poem

magazines. This culminated in his competing, in his last year at Oxford, for the Newdigate Prize Poem, the chief prize for poetry at the University. It was perhaps a little lucky for Wilde that the subject of the poem to be written, decided upon by the authorities, was 'Ravenna', a town which Wilde had visited three years before during his Italian tour, and of which he had retained vivid memories. He won the prize and, in accordance with custom, it was printed at the expense of the University in a small paper-bound edition, thus constituting his first printed book.

Oscar's future was still rather undecided. When Hunter Blair, in his last *Wilde's future* year, asked him what his real ambition in life was, he replied:

'God knows; I won't be an Oxford don anyhow. I'll be a poet, a writer, a dramatist. Somehow or other I'll be famous, and if not famous, I'll be notorious. Or perhaps I'll lead the βίος ἀπολαυστικός [life of pleasure] for a time and then —who knows?—rest and do nothing. What does Plato say is the highest end that man can attain here below? καθεύδειν καὶ ὁρᾶν τὸ ἀγαθόν—to sit down and contemplate the good. Perhaps that will be the end of me too.'

Lily Langtry, 'the Jersey Lily',
adored by Wilde

But the truth probably was that he was a little disappointed at not being offered a Fellowship. Six years of academic life at Trinity, Dublin, and Magdalen, Oxford, had almost got him into a groove from which it might be an effort to escape. His father, Sir William, had died during his second year at Oxford; the Merrion Square establishment had broken up and Speranza had followed her sons to England, to try to establish a *salon* in London on the lines of the one in Dublin. So, after taking his degree, Wilde came to London to see what that city held for him. Sir William had left very little money, but Oscar still had a little of his inheritance. His brother Willie had found a niche in journalism and he helped Oscar in his early struggles, introducing him to editors who published his poems. Oscar shared rooms in London with an old Oxford friend and artist, Frank Miles, who was making his name as the portrayer of beautiful women. Their rooms were at No. 13, Salisbury Street, off the Strand, which was a fashionable residential district at the time. And it was then that Wilde met Lily Langtry, the most celebrated beauty of her day, and of course he fell violently in love with her, as indeed did every man of whom she ever took the slightest notice. Frank Miles made dozens of drawings of her and Oscar wrote her poems, and once Miles exclaimed: 'I with my pencil and Oscar with his pen will make Lily the Gioconda and the Laura of this century.' It was for her that Oscar wrote his poem *The New Helen,* and when his first volume of collected poems was published, he presented her with a copy, on the fly-leaf of which he wrote: 'To Helen, formerly of Troy, but now of London.'

It was now that Oscar Wilde began to have attention called to himself by his unconventional clothing. In his last term at Oxford he had appeared at a fancy dress ball as Prince Rupert and he declared that reformation of dress was of far more importance than a reformation of religion. And now he occasionally went out in the evening in a velvet coat edged with braid, knee-breeches, black silk stockings, a soft loose silk shirt with a wide turn-down collar and a large flowing

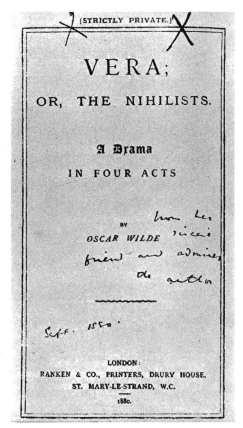

The title-page of *Vera*, Wilde's first play

green tie. This, however, was only done for what would nowadays be called publicity. In his daily life he was always fashionably dressed and never appeared in public except in the 'correct' clothing. The legend that he 'walked down Piccadilly with a poppy or a lily in his medieval hand' is quite untrue, arising from the behaviour of characters in the Gilbert and Sullivan operetta *Patience*; in later life, Wilde always protested against this story. 'Anyone could have done that,' he said; 'the difficult thing to achieve was to make people believe that I had done it.'

Early in 1880, he wrote his first play, *Vera*, centred round Nihilism in Russia. *First play* By this time he was badly in need of money, but he failed to interest any producer in the play. However, the assassination of Tsar Alexander II in March 1881 brought Russia and Russian politics very much to the fore in England, and Mrs Bernard Beere agreed to put the play on at the Adelphi Theatre in December 1881, with herself in the leading part; but the production was cancelled at the

NINCOMPOOPIANA.—THE MUTUAL ADMIRATION SOCIETY.

Satire on the Aesthetic Movement by *Punch* in 1880

last moment. The real reason for the cancellation has never been clearly ascertained; the official announcement in the Press was that 'considering the present state of political feeling in England, Mr Oscar Wilde has decided on postponing, for a time, the production of his drama, *Vera*'. It is more likely, however, as Mr Hesketh Pearson points out in his admirable *Life of Oscar Wilde* (Methuen, London, 1946), that the withdrawal was really in deference to the feelings of the Prince of Wales, who was very friendly disposed towards Wilde, who had met him on several occasions and who was closely related to the late Tsar's widow.

Aesthete and wit   Oscar Wilde's reputation as an eccentric, a wit, and the great apostle of Aestheticism was so widely recognised that as early as 1880 he began to attract the notice of *Punch* which, in February of that year, began its long series of lampoons, caricatures, and general attacks upon him. He also appeared, thinly disguised, in several plays including one, *The Colonel*, by F. C. Burnand, the editor of *Punch*, which had a long run, with Herbert Beerbohm Tree giving a satirical interpretation of Wilde. It is interesting to note that, many years later, Tree played the lead in Wilde's *A Woman of No Importance*. But the

A REACTION IN ÆSTHETICS.

THE SIX-MARK TEA-POT.

Æsthetic Bridegroom. "It is quite consummate, is it not!"
Intense Bride. "It is, indeed! Oh, Algernon, let us live up to it!"

Two more cartoons from *Punch* during 1880. The cartoon on the right was inspired by an epigram of Wilde; 'Algernon' resembles Swinburne

culmination was reached with the production of the Gilbert and Sullivan operetta *Patience,* which first appeared at The Opera Comique in April 1881 and was later transferred to the Savoy Theatre, where it had a brilliant success. The operetta was a skit on Aestheticism in general and, in spite of what many writers have assumed, none of the characters was supposed to represent Wilde who, incidentally, was highly amused by the performance.

'Patience'

As has been the case with so many distinguished writers in the past, Wilde's literary talent was very late in developing, and until his thirtieth year the only book of his that had appeared (apart from the Newdigate Prize Poem, *Ravenna*) was the book of his collected poems published (it is said at his own expense) in 1881. The reception of this book was very mixed and mostly hostile, but it rapidly went into five editions.

Collected poems

Money was getting very scarce indeed and early in 1881 Oscar Wilde and his friend Frank Miles left their luxurious rooms in Salisbury Street and retired to more modest quarters in Keats House, No. 3, Tite Street, the same street in which he was to live from the time of his marriage until the tragic events of 1895. There, at the request of Miss Mary Anderson, the New York actress, he began to write the five-act tragedy which was afterwards to develop into *The Duchess of Padua*. And while negotiations concerning this play were proceeding, he received an offer to go on a lecture tour in America from Colonel F. W. Morse, business manager of Richard D'Oyly Carte, who produced all the Gilbert and Sullivan operettas.

It has often been suggested that he accepted the offer of this American tour with the undeclared motive of advertising *Patience*, and that he received a handsome fee for doing so. This is manifestly untrue. The operetta needed no such advertising; it stood on its own merits and was eagerly looked forward to by the American theatre-going public. Besides, as Walter Hamilton points out in *The Aesthetic Movement in England*, Wilde was 'scarcely the man to become an advertising medium for a play which professed to ridicule everything he held sacred in art and poetry'. No; the reasons that induced him to accept Colonel Morse's offer were twofold: to practise his public speaking on what he hoped would not be too critical an audience, and to try to arrange for the production of *Vera*, in which he still placed great hopes. Incidentally, the financial aspect of the enterprise was not altogether without its inducement!

Wilde left England in the *Arizona* on 24th December 1881, and arrived in New York on 2nd January 1882, declaring that he was 'disappointed in the tame Atlantic'. His ship arrived too late to pass quarantine before sundown, but he was immediately besieged by a group of hostile reporters, anxious to do their worst for 'the poet and apostle of English aestheticism'. Needless to say, all the New York papers carried long stories about him next morning. The description of him that appeared in the *New York Tribune* is worth recording:

'The most striking thing about the poet's appearance is his height, which is several inches over six feet, and the next thing to attract attention is his hair, which is of a dark brown colour, and falls down upon his shoulders. . . . When he laughs his lips part widely and show a shining row of upper teeth, which are superlatively white. The complexion, instead of being of the rosy hue so common in Englishmen, is so utterly devoid of colour that it can only be said to resemble putty. His eyes are blue, or a light grey, and instead of being "dreamy", as some of his admirers have imagined them to be, they are bright and quick—not at all like those of one given to perpetual musing on the ineffably beautiful and true. Instead of having a small delicate hand, only fit to caress a lily, his fingers are long and when doubled up would form a fist that would hit a hard knock, should an occasion arise for the owner to descend to that kind of argument. . . . One of the peculiarities of his speech is that he accents almost at regular intervals without regard to the sense, perhaps as a result of an effort to be rhythmic in conversation as well as in verse.'

Sketches from the first performance of *Patience* ▶

ye indifference of ye Dragoons.

ye flesh-ly poet

ye dairy maid

ye Greenery-Yallery, Grosvenor Gallery one

ye faithful one

2vite too Jolly utter

ye legend of ye Maiden & ye Curate.

Writers of songs and dance-music also joined in making fun of Wilde

When he was asked, on the following morning, if he had anything to declare, he replied: 'Nothing but my genius.'

The Americans refused to take him seriously, perhaps because they could not believe that what they considered to be his posing could possibly be genuine, and therefore thought that he was trying to make fun of them. The Americans of the 1880s were forthright citizens who had not much use for either literature or art, and still less for eccentricities of behaviour, so they regarded Wilde as being little removed from a clown. He was therefore treated as a joke, and one in bad taste at that. But he gave as good as he got, and made many caustic remarks about the American way of life, such as, 'In America, life is one long expectoration'; and 'I believe a most serious problem for the American people to consider is the cultivation of better manners. It is the most noticeable, the most painful, defect in American civilisation.'

While in America he delivered lectures in about seventy different towns all

Wilde lampooned in
pamphlets

over the continent, meeting with a mixed reception from his audiences, but
nearly always a hostile Press. The *Tribune* summed up his tour:

'Wherever he has appeared some new way of enhancing the public's enjoy-
ment has been invented. College students of the University towns found in him
a perfectly justifiable object for their ridicule. Quack doctors hit upon his
favourite sunflower as a means of advertising their own nostrums. . . . In the free
and untrammelled West, tradespeople utilized his form as a means of advertisement, and if Mr Wilde took up a newspaper there, he very likely saw himself,

The Kansas Opera House, where Oscar Wilde lectured during his American tour

dressed in his special garb, standing at the head of an announcement by a clothing dealer that "Wild Oscar, the Ass-thete, buys his clothes of our establishment".'

It says a very great deal for the strength of Oscar's belief in his mission that he never allowed this kind of attack to perturb him and that he always kept his good humour, however embarrassing the situation might be.

One of the main contributory causes of his embarrassment was the attitude of American women, who gushed over him and lionised him, to the infuriation of American men. In a letter to his friend Norman Forbes-Robertson he stated that he employed two secretaries, one for autographs and the other for locks of hair demanded by the ladies. Many reports reached England of the extravagant parties given in his honour. One party in New York was a dinner of about twenty people, all of whom, with the exception of the host and Oscar Wilde, were ladies well known for their wit and beauty. That sort of thing was inclined to create a bad atmosphere round Wilde, who was already not regarded in too good a light by the male population of America. He was undoubtedly spoiled

Oscar Wilde's headquarters in New York, next to Washington Irving's house

and his posing and affectation counted very much against him. Yet his American tour was, on the whole, a brilliant success, and he returned to England in January 1883 covered, if not with glory, at least with considerable notoriety.

His final summing up of America is contained in two statements which have become so well known that one hesitates to repeat them: 'When good Americans die, they go to Paris; when bad Americans die they stay in America.' And when he heard that Rossetti had given some importunate hanger-on enough money to go to America, he observed: 'Of course, if one had enough money to go to America one would not go.'

Wilde's return from America brought him back to earth. In spite of the attitude of rather amused tolerance which he affected towards the New World, he certainly missed all the fêting and flattery that had been heaped upon him in the course of his lecture tour. He was back in the cold, hard, matter-of-fact atmosphere of England. The velvet jacket, the knee-breeches, and all the panoply of Aestheticism were outmoded and had to be discarded. For the first two months after his return he was in demand at parties in London where he entertained the

Oscar Wilde figuring in an advertisement in an
American paper for a pirated performance of
Patience with which he had no connection whatever

George Maxwell Robeson, a Congressman who became attracted to Aestheticism

company with tales of America, explaining to them that really Americans 'had everything in common with English people except, of course, the language'. But eventually this palled, Oscar became depressed and late in February he packed his bags and went to Paris, where he engaged rooms in the Hôtel Voltaire, on the Quai Voltaire.

It was here that Wilde encountered Robert Sherard. When they first met they felt that they had nothing in common and disliked each other intensely; but they gradually got together and became life-long friends. Sherard wrote the first three biographical studies of Wilde, after his death: *Oscar Wilde, the Story of an Unhappy Friendship, The Real Oscar Wilde*, and *The Life of Oscar Wilde*. On these three books are based all the other biographies of Wilde, except the so-called biography by Frank Harris, which is nothing else but the self-glorification of Frank Harris. Sherard got a great deal of his material from Lady Wilde when she was a very old lady and was inclined to let her imagination run away with her, particularly where the family history was concerned; and Sherard, a born journalist, was much more attracted by the interest of a story than by its accuracy, a failing which we can see running through all his books. But where his actual contact with Wilde is concerned, he is quite reliable, and he gives a vivid picture of his manner of living in Paris at that time:

Paris

Wilde, in the dress of an aesthete, photographed
in Alabama in June 1882

'In the daytime, when he was at work, he dressed in a white dressing-gown fashioned after the monkish cowl that Balzac used to wear at his writing table. At that time he was modelling himself on Balzac. Beside the dressing-gown, he had acquired an ivory cane with a head of turquoises, which was a replica of the famous walking-stick which Honoré de Balzac used to carry when love had transformed the recluse into a fop. But he was not borrowing from the master these foibles of toilette alone. I think that at that time he was striving in earnest to school himself into labour and production. He was sated with social success, and had fixed a high ambition to carve out for himself a great place in English letters. He had inspired himself with that passage in *La Cousine Bette* in which Balzac declares that constant labour is the law of art as it is the law of life, and points to the fact that all great artists have been unresting workers.'

The Paris boulevards as Wilde first saw them in 1883

One of Wilde's main objects in retiring to Paris was to finish off *The Duchess of Padua*, the play that he had undertaken to write for Miss Mary Anderson before his lecture tour in America. He had probably started to write this play during his American tour and worked on it in London on his return to England, but the matter had now become urgent, as he had signed an agreement by which he committed himself to delivering the play by 1st March 1883. The play was actually completed on 15th March, very shortly after his arrival in Paris, and was immediately dispatched to America. It was of the utmost importance to Wilde that the play should meet with Mary Anderson's approval, as he had already had an advance of a thousand dollars from her, and she had promised a further advance of four thousand dollars on account of royalties, if and when the play was accepted. He therefore cabled to America as soon as he

'The Duchess of Padua'

41

Robert Harborough Sherard,
Wilde's earliest biographer

calculated that the play would have arrived there; but the reply was a blunt
refusal and poor Oscar's hopes of affluence, however temporary, were rudely
shattered. Sherard was with him when the cable came, but he made only two
references to what was really a disaster to him. 'This is rather tedious, Robert,' he
exclaimed when he read the cable; and that evening he observed, rather rue-
fully, 'We shan't be able to dine with the Duchess tonight.'

Although Oscar was mortified by this set-back to his fortunes, he did not
allow it to depress him unduly, and retained his self-confidence. He probably
realised that the play was not a good one and that it did not do him justice; many
years later he admitted this to Robert Ross, observing that it was the only one of
his writings that was 'really unfit for publication'. It was, after all, only a 'pot-
boiler', written in order to provide enough money to enable him to settle down
to more congenial work. The play is, nevertheless, included in all the collected
editions of Wilde's works. It was once produced in Germany, without any
success; the only other production was at the Broadway Theatre, New York,
where it ran for three weeks in 1891, without the author's name and under the
title of *Guido Ferranti*.

Mary Anderson at the age of
twenty-four in 1883, when
Oscar wrote a play for her,
The Duchess of Padua,
which she refused to accept

He remained in Paris for two more months, idling the time away and enjoying his life. He met all the most distinguished French authors and artists of the period. Among them were Victor Hugo, Paul Verlaine, Mallarmé, Henri de Régnier, Jean Richepin, Paul Bourget, Degas, Pissarro, and Coquelin. He found Verlaine stupid, degenerate, besotted and, which was worse in his eyes, very ugly. Wilde had a horror of ugliness in any form, and one well-known epigram of his ran: 'It is better to be beautiful than to be good, but it is better to be good than to be ugly.' He was no more successful with Zola, who could not understand him; on one occasion Zola had to propose the toast of 'The Arts', coupled with Oscar's name. He concluded his speech with: 'Unfortunately, Mr. Wilde will be obliged to reply in his own barbarous language.' This was, of course, said in French: Wilde rose and began his speech also in French, saying: 'I am Irish by birth and English by adoption so that I am condemned, as Monsieur Zola says, to speak in the language of Shakespeare.'

Apart from finishing *The Duchess of Padua,* the only work Wilde appears to have done during this Paris visit was to write *The Harlot's House,* which was subsequently printed in *The Dramatic Review,* and to continue to work on his

French authors and artists

Paul Verlaine, whom Wilde met in 1883 during his visit to Paris

Victor Hugo, another of the famous whom Wilde met in Paris

poem *The Sphinx,* the idea for which had first come to him at Oxford, and at which he worked intermittently for ten years before it was published.

Return to London   When Wilde returned to London in May 1883, his first act was to pawn his Berkeley Gold Medal, in order to get the wherewithal to live. During the previous three months he had spent what was left of the proceeds of the American venture, and he had earned nothing; so he called on Colonel Morse, who had arranged his American tour, and Morse arranged another lecture tour for him through England and Scotland for the autumn and winter. Before starting this, however, Wilde paid another visit to America to be present at the rehearsals of *Vera,* which the American actress Marie Prescott was producing. It was put on at the Union Square Theatre in New York on 20th August 1883. The play ran for only one week, but Marie Prescott still had faith in it and tried to persuade Oscar to come on tour with it, playing the leading part of Prince Paul himself. No doubt Oscar was tempted by this suggestion, which must have appealed to his love of the incongruous, but he was committed to his lecture tour in England and had reluctantly to decline.

Emile Zola: a portrait by Manet ▶

Miners of Leadville, Colorado. 'The only well-dressed men,' said Wilde, 'I have seen in America'

One of the first lectures he delivered was one that subsequently proved to be a very popular one, on his 'Personal Impressions of America'. It was delivered at Princes' Hall, in Piccadilly; one London paper, reporting the lecture, remarked on the 'undercurrent of Irish fun and the curiously amusing fashion of presenting vivid sketches of the men and women and mountains and rivers and theatres and teacups and magnolias and moons and girls which he had observed on the other side of the Atlantic'.

Among other places in which he had lectured in America was Leadville, in the Rocky Mountains, where the costume of his audience, which consisted almost entirely of miners, appealed strongly to him; the majority of them wore red shirts, corduroy trousers, and high boots; and afterwards he said that in all his journeys through the country the only well-dressed men that he saw were these Western miners. His own descriptions of his reception by them is typical of his 'Impressions of America':

'I spoke to them of the early Florentines, and they slept as though no crime had

And a caricature of him
explaining why

ever stained the ravines of their mountain home. I described to them the
pictures of Botticelli and the name, which seemed to them like a new drink,
roused them from their dreams. I read them passages from the autobiography of
Benvenuto Cellini, and they seemed much delighted. I was reproved by my
hearers for not having brought him with me. I explained that he had been dead
for some little time, which elicited the enquiry, "Who shot him?" I had almost
won them to reverence for what is beautiful in art when unluckily I described
one of Whistler's "nocturnes in blue and gold". Then they leapt to their feet and
swore that such things should not be. Some of the younger ones pulled out their
revolvers and left to see if Whistler was prowling about the saloons. Had he
been there, so bitter was their feeling that I fear he would have been killed.'

It was at about this time that Oscar Wilde and James McNeill Whistler
became great friends. But the friendship was a short-lived one. Whistler was
twenty years older than Wilde, and had for years held a unique position in
London as a raconteur and a wit; but he now began to find himself being ousted

*James McNeill
Whistler*

47

The huge Mormon Tabernacle in which Wilde lectured in Salt Lake City. He wrote: 'It holds with ease fourteen families'

A balloon car, the type of public conveyance common at the time of Wilde's visit to America

James McNeill Whistler

from his position by the younger man, and this made him very bitter. He continually accused Wilde of plagiarism and when one day, following some quip of Whistler's, Wilde observed: 'I wish I had said that!', Whistler retorted: 'You will, Oscar, you will!' But the real coolness between the two men began with a long review by Wilde in the *Pall Mall Gazette* of Whistler's 'Ten o'Clock' lecture. Wilde had attended the lecture and his article appeared the next day; it was well calculated to infuriate Whistler by its sarcasm. He wrote:

'Mr Whistler was relentless and, with charming ease and much grace of manner, explained to the public that the only thing they should cultivate was ugliness, and that on their permanent stupidity rested all the hope of art in the future. The scene was in every way delightful; he stood there, a miniature Mephistopheles, mocking the majority! He was like a brilliant surgeon lecturing to a class composed of subjects destined ultimately for dissection, and solemnly assuring them how valuable to science their maladies were and how absolutely uninteresting the slightest symptoms of health on their part would be.'

Oscar Wilde on his return
from America in 1883

The article ended: 'That Mr Whistler is indeed one of the greatest masters of painting, is my opinion. And I may add that in this opinion Mr Whistler himself entirely concurs.'

There followed a correspondence of a very acrimonious nature, in which they insulted each other ruthlessly. Whistler reproduced most of this correspondence in *The Gentle Art of Making Enemies*: but they never spoke to each other again.

Oscar Wilde soon became weary of lecturing and being billed as 'The Great Aesthete', and of the people who came to hear him merely out of curiosity, in the hope that he would be wearing 'funny clothes'. It was, besides, an unsettled life, with the constant moving from place to place. So, after delivering about sixty lectures, he returned to London determined to make his living by his pen. In *Wilde engaged* November 1883, in the middle of his tour, his engagement had been announced to Miss Constance Mary Lloyd, the daughter of a well-known Irish barrister, Horace Lloyd, QC, who had died at a comparatively early age. Her mother had married again and Constance herself was living in Lancaster Gate, London, at the time, with her paternal grandfather. Constance's maternal grandmother, who lived at No. 1, Ely Place, in Dublin, knew the Wildes very well, and it was

Constance Mary Wilde (*née* Lloyd), Oscar's wife

The 'little church round the corner', where Oscar Wilde was married

through another daughter of hers that Oscar first met her, probably in 1881. However that may be, there is the authority of Constance's brother, Otho Lloyd, to support the fact that Oscar proposed to Constance in the Ely Place house in November 1883.

Wilde's marriage   They were married on 29th May 1884 at St James's Church, Paddington, this being the church of the parish in which Lancaster Gate lay, and a reception was held afterwards at her grandfather's house there. The honeymoon was spent in Paris at the Hôtel Wagram in the Rue de Rivoli. It was here that Sherard first met Constance, and he gives the following account of the meeting:

'The Wildes were staying in some very pleasant rooms on one of the higher stories of the hotel, and a beautiful pair they made. The lovely young wife seemed supremely happy. There was bright sunlight, as one only sees it in Paris, on the Tuileries without, yet the room where I first met Constance was just as

16, Tite Street, Chelsea;
Wilde's home during the
whole of his married life

gladsome. It was full of flowers and youth and laughter. And as I walked out with Oscar, he told me that marriage was indeed wonderful. We were passing through the Marché St Honoré at the time, and here he stopped and rifled a flower-stall of its loveliest blooms and sent them, with a word of love on his card, to the bride whom he had quitted but a moment before.'

But this Garden of Eden could not last for ever, and the stern realities of life had to be faced; so the Wildes returned to London and went to live in Oscar's bachelor rooms in Charles Street, while the house they had taken in Chelsea, No. 16, Tite Street, was being got ready for them. Constance Wilde had a *Wilde's house* fairly generous allowance of some few hundreds a year from her Lloyd grandfather, who was becoming a very old man, and this enabled the young couple to have the house decorated and furnished in accordance with their own, or rather Oscar's own, particular taste. The general scheme of decoration was arranged by the well-known architect E. W. Godwin, who was partly responsible for the London Law Courts. Godwin was assisted in his task by Whistler, with whom Wilde had not yet quarrelled.

The house was a small one, and followed the pattern of nearly every middle-class house built in the mid-Victorian era; that is to say, four or five floors, with two rooms on each floor, varying in size with the size of the house. On the ground floor, Oscar Wilde's study occupied the front room; there was then a fairly spacious hall, beyond which lay the dining-room, looking out over a small garden at the back.

On the first floor, the drawing-room occupied the front of the house, while at the back there was a kind of Oriental lounge which served as a smoking-room, a spare room when guests were staying the night, or a dressing-room for Wilde. The rest of the house was taken up with bedrooms and, in due course, nurseries.

The colour scheme of Oscar Wilde's study on the ground floor was red and yellow, the walls being painted pale primrose and the woodwork red. A cast of the Hermes of Praxiteles stood on a red column in a corner by the window. A

Mrs Stella Patrick Campbell.
A portrait study by Charles
Haslewood Shannon, RA

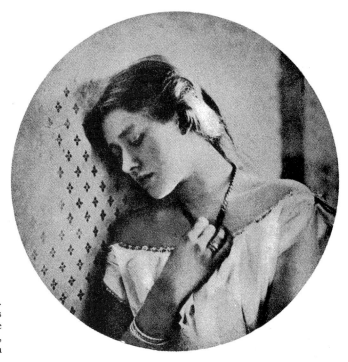

Ellen Terry.
A study of the most famous
actress of her day by the
most artistic photographer,
Julia Margaret Cameron

few small pictures adorned the walls: a Simeon Solomon, a Monticelli, and a delicate drawing of Mrs Patrick Campbell, the famous actress, by Aubrey Beardsley. Apart from these, and a large writing-desk which had once belonged to Thomas Carlyle, the room was furnished entirely with books; Greek and Latin Classics, French literature and presentation copies of contemporary European authors predominated. It was here, in an atmosphere of cigarette smoke, that most of Wilde's serious work was done, and it was from here that hooligans and souvenir-hunters stole everything they could lay hands upon when he lay in prison, a bankrupt, and his property was sold in a mockery of a public auction, and the brokers were completely indifferent to what happened. Even letters from Constance Wilde were looted and sold many years later.

The prevailing note in the dining-room at the back of the house was white, blending with pale blue and yellow, the carpet and dining-room chairs being white, the walls white picked out with blue and the sideboard and other furniture yellow.

But it was on the drawing-room on the first floor that the greatest thought and care had been lavished. The main attraction here was the ceiling, designed by Whistler, into which peacocks' feathers had been inserted. The walls were

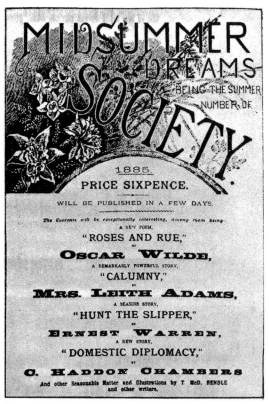

A weekly journal 'for the Upper and Middle Classes' to which Wilde contributed

hung with etchings by Whistler and Mortimer Menpes, except the one on the right of the door, on which hung a full-length oil painting of Wilde by an American admirer, Harper Pennington. A painted grand piano stood in one corner of the room, occupying a disproportionately large area of it. Bamboo chairs painted black and white, tall vases containing bulrushes and small tables covered with bric-à-brac and *objets d'art* took up much of the floor space; but even so the room was not so cluttered up as were most of the drawing-rooms of the period.

The drawing-room was at the back of the house, above the dining-room. The only other place in the house which showed the influence of Godwin and Whistler was the room above Oscar's study, at the front of the house, which has already been mentioned. Heavy curtains draped the windows, giving the room a rather mysterious look. The walls were lined with a peculiar embossed paper called lincrusta-walton, with a William Morris pattern of dark red and dull gold. The general décor was a mixture of the Far East and Morocco, with divans and a glass bead curtain before the door. The main use of this room was for relaxation and smoking; it also served as a spare room for guests.

The Private View of the Academy, 1881, by Frith

The rest of the house contained bedrooms and nurseries and therefore was very much like any house of the time, but the living rooms had a very definite character of their own and it was in these that the Wildes entertained celebrities from almost every walk of life. To Mrs Wilde's receptions came people of such widely differing interests as Arthur Balfour, Sarah Bernhardt, Mark Twain, John Sargent, Robert Browning, John Bright, Sir William Richmond, Ellen Terry, Algernon Charles Swinburne, Lady de Grey, Lily Langtry, Herbert Beerbohm Tree, and John Ruskin, to mention only a very few.

Oscar and Constance Wilde settled in to the Tite Street house and Oscar began to look round to decide what to do next. He was now thirty years of age, married, his name known to everyone, with extravagant tastes, no money, no fixed occupation. Constance's dowry was not sufficient to provide even the bare necessities of existence. Oscar had really achieved nothing so far but a reputation as a conversationalist and a great deal of notoriety; *Punch* was still relentlessly pursuing him with caricatures and lampoons. Frith had exhibited his now famous picture entitled 'The Private View of the Royal Academy, 1881' with Oscar as one of the principal figures, and this too brought down the wrath of

Early married life

Robert Browning and Mark Twain, both frequent visitors to the Tite Street house

Punch. But these things did not pay the rent and the tradesmen's bills so, almost in desperation, and certainly much against his will, he undertook another lecture tour of the United Kingdom. Even this form of activity did not bring in sufficient money to make ends meet: in those days, there were no fat expense accounts upon which a lecturer or a business man could draw, thereby keeping all his fees to himself. An illustration of the Wilde ménage difficulties is contained in the story of Oscar being approached one day in Tite Street by a tax collector: the following conversation ensued:

'I want to talk to you about your taxes.'

'What taxes? What makes you think I should pay taxes?'

'Well, sir, you live in this house and sleep here!'

'Ah, yes! But then, you see, I sleep so badly!'

Reviewing the situation, one must come to the conclusion that for the first four years of their married life things were in a pretty bad way. Even the notoriety seemed to be on the wane. However, early in 1885, Oscar got a job reviewing books for the *Pall Mall Gazette,* which had the effect of slightly relieving the

pressure. Owing to the indefatigable industry and research of Stuart Mason, all the reviews that Oscar wrote for this and other papers have been identified and preserved in the twelfth volume of the first collected edition of Oscar Wilde's works, published by his literary executor, Robert Ross, in 1908. In his introduction to this book of reviews, Ross says:

'From these reviews which illustrate the middle period of Wilde's meteoric career, between the aesthetic period and the production of *Lady Windermere's Fan,* we learn *his* opinion of the contemporaries who thought little enough of him. That he revised many of these opinions, notably those that are harsh, I need scarcely say; and after his release from prison he lost much of his admiration for certain writers.'

At about the same time that Wilde started his literary criticisms for the *Pall Mall Gazette,* he also performed a similar service, that of dramatic critic, to the *Dramatic Review.* But even these activities did not bring him enough money to live in comfort, particularly as in June 1885 the expenses of his household were increased by the birth of his elder son, Cyril. However, in 1887 he was appointed editor of a monthly magazine entitled *The Lady's World.* At first, Wilde did not himself contribute to the magazine, but five months after he became editor the magazine was enlarged and renamed *The Woman's World,* and he wrote regularly for it in the form of 'Literary Notes', being reviews at some length of

Vignette from *The Woman's World,* edited by Oscar Wilde

It was the age of bazaars; Constance Wilde supervising a stall at one of them

contemporary literature and art of all descriptions. Some idea of the scope of his criticisms can be gathered from the names of the authors and artists with whose work he dealt. Among well over two hundred names appeared those of Alfred Austin, Wilfrid Blunt, Randolph Caldecott, Edward Carpenter, Stephen Coleridge, the Hon. John Collier, Walter Crane, Adam Lindsay Gordon, Bret Harte, William Ernest Henley, Richard le Gallienne, Professor Mahaffy, Edith Nesbit, Ouida, Walter Pater, George Saintsbury, Algernon Charles Swinburne, Walt Whitman, John Strange Winter, and W. B. Yeats.

When Wilde first worked for *The Woman's World*, he was like a child with a new toy. He always took a keen delight at any new departure in his life, and he thoroughly enjoyed the feeling of importance that his editorship gave him. His wide circle of friends and acquaintances was invaluable to him in his search for contributors; among the people whom he persuaded to write for his paper were Princess Christian, 'Carmen Sylva' (Queen of Roumania), Ouida, Oscar Browning, and Olive Schreiner. He was less successful with Sarah Bernhardt, whom he tried to persuade to sign a 'History of My Teagown', offering to write the article himself; but she decided that it was taking too great a risk. Then he tried to persuade Sarah to write her impressions of her American tour; as,

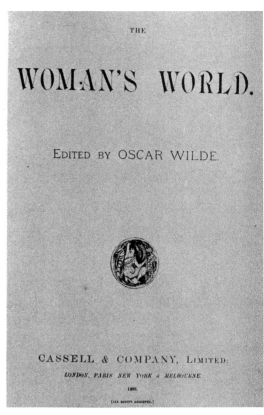

Victorian taste in décor—The Hall—from *The Woman's World*   The title-page

however, she was contemplating a return tour in the near future, and Oscar wanted her to be, to say the least of it, not too flattering to the American people, she prudently declined.

After the novelty of this new venture wore off, Wilde found the discipline of having to go to an office every day at the same time very irksome, and in June 1889, exactly two years after he had become editor of *The Woman's World*, he resigned from the appointment. The magazine survived him for only one further year.

It must not be supposed that during his two years with *The Woman's World* he devoted all his energies to the publication of the magazine. He wrote occasional poems. In 1887 he wrote and had published four short stories, 'Lord Arthur Savile's Crime', 'The Canterville Ghost', 'Lady d'Alroy' (afterwards renamed 'The Sphinx without a Secret') and 'A Model Millionaire'; these were afterwards collected and published in 1891 under the title of *Lord Arthur Savile's Crime and Other Stories*. These stories are as popular today as when

Short stories

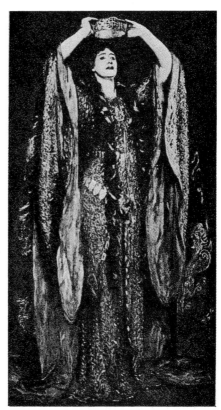

A contribution by Beatrice Crane · Ellen Terry as Lady Macbeth

they were written; there have been at least three dramatic versions of the first one, and film versions have been made of that and of 'The Canterville Ghost'.

At the same time, he was writing the fairy stories that were published in 1888 under the title *The Happy Prince and Other Tales*. These stories have now joined those of Perrault, Hans Andersen, and Grimm as being among the great fairy stories of the world. They are almost more in the nature of poems in prose than stories, particularly 'The Nightingale and the Rose', which some years ago was made the motif of a very beautiful ballet. After 1886 Oscar wrote very little poetry until the end of his life, when he wrote *The Ballad of Reading Gaol*. This was probably because he thought that he could give rein to his urge for writing poetry more successfully and more readily through the medium of prose. So that in *The Happy Prince*, and in the stories collected in one volume and published in 1891 under the title of *A House of Pomegranates,* he adopted a style which was half way between romantic prose and blank verse; this is particularly apparent

'The Happy Prince and other Tales'

Constance Wilde and her elder
son Cyril, another study by the
Cameron Studios

when the stories are read aloud, as it is impossible to read them intelligently
without a certain lilt and cadence.

The year 1891 was one of great industry, so far as Wilde was concerned; for,
in addition to *A House of Pomegranates*, he published three other books. *Lord
Arthur Savile's Crime* has already been mentioned. The others were *Intentions* and
The Picture of Dorian Gray, which had appeared in an abbreviated form in
Lippincott's Monthly Magazine in July of the previous year.

'Intentions'   *Intentions* consisted of four brilliant essays which had previously appeared in
The Nineteenth Century and *The Fortnightly Review*. While they might have been
missed when they were first published, they created a considerable stir when they
came out in book form and so attracted the attention of the reviewers. Although
the essays were serious in their philosophy and in the message they strove to
convey, there was a note of frivolity about them that infuriated the staid and

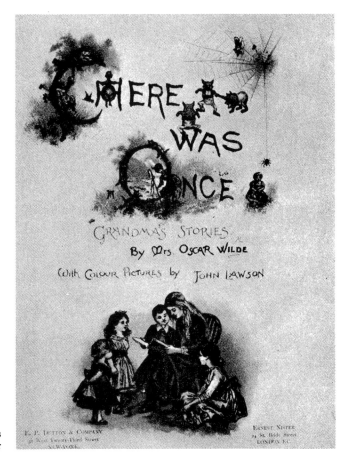

Mrs Oscar Wilde, too, was
a writer

conventional critic. *The Athenaeum* went so far as to accuse Oscar of having '*deliberately* resorted to tricks of the smart advertiser in order to attract attention to his wares'. On the other hand, a most favourable review was given to the book by *The Speaker*, a magazine by no means given to praising any writing in which it detected signs of unconventionality:

'A book like this, with its curious convolutions of sentiment, its intricacies of mood and manner, its masquerade of disguises, cannot possibly receive adequate notice in the space of a brief review. Mr Wilde is always suggestive; he is interesting even when he is provoking. At his best, when he is most himself—a master of epigram—he can be admirable even when his eloquence reminds us of the eloquent writing of others. He is conscious of the charm of graceful echoes, and is always original in his quotations. Over and over again he proves to us the truth of masks.'

The last words of the foregoing extract refer to the title of one of the four essays of which the book is composed, namely 'The Truth of Masks'. The other three are 'Pen, Pencil and Poison', 'The Decay of Lying', and 'The Critic as Artist'. The first of these is a study of Thomas Griffiths Wainewright, of whom Oscar says that 'though of an extremely artistic temperament, he followed many masters other than Art, being not only a poet and painter, an art-critic, an antiquarian and a writer of prose, an amateur of beautiful things, and a dilettante of things delightful, but also a forger of no mean or ordinary capabilities, and as a subtle and secret poisoner almost without rival in this or any age.' Wainewright's personality fascinated Wilde, who recognised so much of his own character in him; at the same time, he tried to probe into the criminal side of his character and to reconcile the two utterly incompatible sides.

'The Critic as Artist' occupies considerably more than half the book; it had as its sub-title 'with some remarks upon the importance of doing nothing'. It is curious how the word 'importance' seems to run through Oscar Wilde's works: it occurs in the titles of two of his plays, and is constantly cropping up in his essays; it is almost as though the word held a strange sonorousness for him and that he liked to roll it, if not round his tongue, then round his mind. This essay is a very serious and learned disquisition upon the function of criticism and the influence it has exerted upon writers and authors throughout the ages.

'*The Decay of Lying*' But by far the most interesting and entertaining essay in the book is 'The Decay of Lying', in which Oscar has really given his imagination its head. The essay is in the form of a dialogue between two mythical characters named Cyril and Vivian; these were the names of Oscar's two sons, but as they were only six and four and a half at the time the book was published, they could scarcely be held responsible for the opinions expressed in the essay. The dominant theme of the essay is the vast superiority of Art over Nature, leading up to the conclusion that Nature follows Art and adopts whatever the highest Art has to teach her. Vivian has written an essay called 'The Decay of Lying' and is discussing it with Cyril, who shows signs of disapprobation. Vivian reads passages from his essay, and this is where Oscar is really in his element and falls back into the mood that inspired *The Happy Prince* and *A House of Pomegranates*:

'Art finds her own perfection within, and not outside of, herself. She is not to be judged by any external standard of resemblance. She is a veil, rather than a mirror. She has flowers that no forests know of, birds that no woodland possesses. She makes and unmakes many worlds, and can draw the moon from heaven with a scarlet thread. Hers are the "forms more real than living man", and hers the great archetypes of which things that have existence are but unfinished copies. Nature has, in her eyes, no laws, no uniformity. She can work

Oscar Wilde, a study
in concentration, by
William Speed, 1888

miracles at her will, and when she calls monsters from the deep they come. She can bid the almond-tree blossom in winter, and send the snow upon the ripe cornfield. At her word the frost lays its silver finger on the burning mouth of June, and the winged lions creep out from the hollows of the Lydian hills. The dryads peer from the thicket as she passes by, and the brown fauns smile strangely at her when she comes near them. She has hawk-faced gods that worship her, and the centaurs gallop at her side.'

'. . . and the centaurs gallop at her side.' Oscar Wilde, without a doubt, could hear the thundering of their hooves as he wrote that passage. In it is contained all the world of make-believe and fantasy that he had built around himself, so that he might live in it as in a golden shell lined with mother of pearl. It was Art, but not artificiality that inspired all Wilde's work; one of the most outstanding characteristics of his work was that it never followed a set pattern, but just followed the mood and inspiration of the moment. What, for instance, could be so remote from the above as the bandying of words and epigrams in *The Importance of Being Earnest,* and the rugged terror which pervades *The Ballad of Reading Gaol?*

Because of the importance of these characteristics when considering Oscar's

Frank Harris, author of *Oscar Wilde: His Life and Confessions* (1930)

mentality, it seems to be worth while to quote another passage from 'The Decay of Lying'. Vivian is reading the end of his essay to Cyril:

'The solid stolid British intellect lies in the desert sands like the Sphinx in Flaubert's *La Chimère,* dances round it, and calls to it with her false, flute-toned voice. It may not hear her now, but surely some day, when we are all bored to death with the commonplace character of modern fiction.

'And when that day dawns, or sunset reddens, how joyous we shall all be! Facts will be regarded as discreditable, Truth will be found mourning over her fetters, and Romance, with her temper of wonder, will return to the land. The very aspect of the world will change to our startled eyes. Out of the sea will rise Behemoth and Leviathan, and sail round the high-pooped galleys, as they do on the delightful maps of those ages when books on geography were actually readable. Dragons will wander about the waste places, and the phoenix will soar from her nest of fire into the air. We shall lay our hands upon the basilisk, and see the jewel in the toad's head. Champing his gilded oats, the Hippogriff will stand in our stalls, and over our heads will float the Blue Bird singing of beautiful and impossible things, of things that are lovely and that never happen, of things that are not and that should be. But before this comes to pass we must cultivate the lost art of Lying.'

In the same year, 1891, *The Picture of Dorian Gray* was published. The idea of this novel had first come to Oscar Wilde some years before. Hesketh Pearson tells the story in his *Life of Oscar Wilde* (Methuen, London, 1946):

'The Picture of Dorian Gray'

'In the year 1884 Wilde used often to drop in at the studio of a painter, Basil Ward, one of whose sitters was a young man of exceptional beauty. . . . When the portrait was done and the youth had gone, Wilde happened to say, "What a pity that such a glorious creature should ever grow old!" The artist agreed, adding, "How delightful it would be if he could remain exactly as he is, while the portrait aged and withered in his stead!" Wilde expressed his obligation by naming the painter in his story "Basil Hallward".'

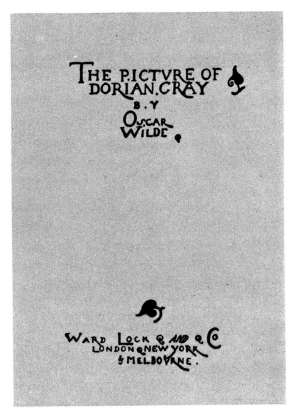

Title-page of the first complete edition of *The Picture of Dorian Gray*

If *Intentions* had irritated the reviewers by its unconventional approach to matters upon which British opinion was supposed to be standardised, the appearance of *Dorian Gray* in book form brought a veritable tornado of abuse whirling round the head of its author, who, in spite of his protests, was secretly delighted by its hostile reception. Even the cover of the book, designed by Charles Ricketts, did not conform to the pattern of book production which the reviewers had been schooled to accept.

The English Press was almost unanimous in its condemnation of the book. The ostensible objection was that it was prurient, immoral, vicious, coarse, and crude. But the real reason for the attack was that it did so much to expose the hypocrisy of Victorian Englishmen who, living in one of the most vicious cities in the world, kept priding themselves, sanctimoniously, upon their virtue. London in the 1880s and 1890s was far more steeped in vice than Paris, at which England and the English Press kept pointing a finger of scorn. Parisians, on the other hand, took their vices so lightly that they became reduced to the proportion of peccadilloes, and in this respect were envied by the English. Another reason for the journalistic anger was that the book did not follow the recognised pattern of the accepted form of fiction, and was therefore incomprehensible to Fleet Street. The *Daily Chronicle*, which had always been 'anti-Wilde', produced the following lucubration: 'It is a tale spawned from the leprous literature of the French *décadents*—a poisonous book, the atmosphere of which is heavy with the mephitic odours of moral and spiritual putrefaction.'

Today, accusations of this sort are what every author longs for, as they are a guarantee of a sale of at least 20,000 copies. But in Victorian days they would stop the sales of any book, as no one would dare to be seen with it, and it was read in secrecy, probably by candle-light, with a view to seeking out obscene passages. How such readers must have been disappointed in reading *The Picture of Dorian Gray!*

Oscar defended his book vigorously in letters to the Press, notably in the *St James's Gazette*, the *Daily Chronicle*, and the *Scots Observer*. The letters are too long to be given in full, but a few extracts may be of interest to those who read the book for the first time. They give an insight into that undercurrent of Victorian hypocrisy which Oscar was continually trying to bring to the surface so as to expose it. The dominant note in his defence of the book was the insistence on his oft-repeated assertion that a work of art cannot be judged by any standard of morality, or by any ethical code, with which it has nothing in common; it is either well or badly executed. The following extracts are all from Oscar's letters printed in the *St James's Gazette*.

'. . . I am quite incapable of understanding how any work of art can be criticised

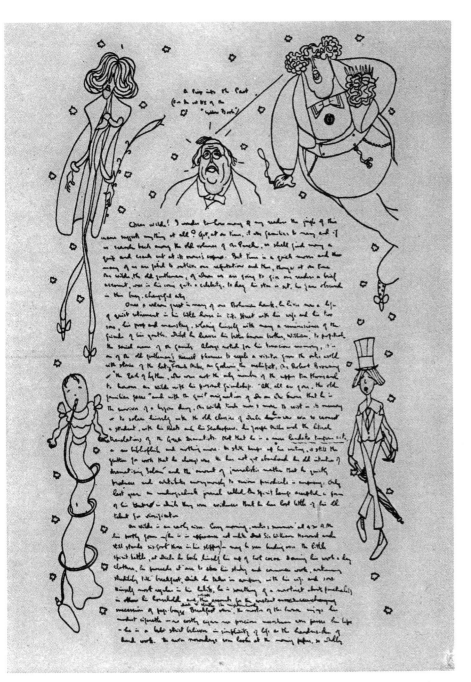

A Peep into the Past was a humorous essay on Oscar Wilde by his life-long friend Max Beerbohm, written as if in the distant future

Edward Carson, who led for the defence
at the trial of the Marquess of Queensberry

from a moral standpoint. The sphere of art and the sphere of ethics are absolutely distinct and separate; and it is to the confusion between the two that we owe the appearance of Mrs Grundy, that amusing old lady who represents the only original form of humour that the middle classes of this country have been able to produce.

'In your issue of today you state that my brief letter published in your columns is the "best reply" I can make to your article upon *Dorian Gray*. This is not so. I do not propose to discuss the matter fully here, but I feel bound to say that your article contains the most unjustifiable attack that has been made upon any man of letters for many years. The writer of it, who is quite incapable of concealing his personal malice, and so in some measure destroys the effect he wishes to produce, seems not to have the slightest idea of the temper in which a work of art should be approached. To say that such a book as mine should be "chucked into the fire" is silly. That is what one does with newspapers.

'The writer of the article suggests that I, in common with that great and noble artist Count Tolstoi, take pleasure in a subject because it is dangerous. About such a suggestion there is this to be said. Romantic art deals with the exception and with the individual. Good people, belonging as they do to the normal, and so commonplace, type, are artistically uninteresting.

'Bad people are, from the point of view of art, fascinating studies. They represent colour, variety and strangeness. Good people exasperate one's reason; bad people stir one's imagination. Your critic, if I must give him so honourable a title, states that the people in my story have no counterpart in life; that they are, to use his vigorous if somewhat vulgar phrase, "mere catchpenny revelations of the non-existent". Quite so. If they existed they would not be worth writing about. The function of the artist is to invent, not to chronicle. There are no such people. If there were I would not write about them. Life, by its realism, is always spoiling the subject-matter of art.

'The poor public, hearing, from an authority so high as your own, that this is a wicked book that should be suppressed, will no doubt rush to it and read it. But alas! they will find that it is a story with a moral. And the moral is this: All excess, as well as all renunciation, brings its own punishment. Yes, there is a terrible moral in *Dorian Gray*—a moral which the prurient will not be able to find in it, but which will be revealed to all whose minds are healthy. Is this an artistic error? I fear it is. It is the only error in the book.

The last portrait of Oscar Wilde before the 1895 disaster

'Finally, Sir, allow me to say this. Such an article as you have published really makes me despair of the possibility of any general culture in England. Were I a French author, and my book were brought out in Paris, there is not a single literary critic in France on any paper of high standing who would think for a moment of criticising it from an ethical standpoint. If he did so he would stultify himself, not merely in the eyes of all men of letters, but in the eyes of the majority of the public.

'You have yourself often spoken against Puritanism. Believe me, Sir, Puritanism is never so offensive and destructive as when it deals with art matters. It is there that it is radically wrong. It is this Puritanism, to which your critic has given expression, that is always marring the artistic instinct of the English. So far from encouraging it, you should set yourself against it, and should try to teach your critics to recognise the essential difference between art and life.

'The gentleman who criticised my book is in a perfectly hopeless confusion about it, and your attempt to help him out by proposing that the subject-matter of art should be limited does not mend matters. It is proper that limitation should be placed on action. It is not proper that limitation should be placed on art. To art belong all things that are and all things that are not, and even the editor of a London paper has no right to restrain the freedom of art in the selection of subject-matter.'

Five years later, Oscar Wilde was to defend *Dorian Gray* again, at the Old Bailey, when the following passage of arms took place between him and his old rival at Trinity College, Dublin, Edward Carson, who appeared for the defence in the case of Regina *v.* Queensberry:

Carson: You are of opinion, I believe, that there is no such thing as an immoral book?

Wilde: Yes.

Carson: Am I right in saying that you do not consider the effect in creating morality or immorality?

Wilde: Certainly I do not.

Carson: So far as your works are concerned, you pose as not being concerned about morality or immorality?

Wilde: I do not know whether you use the word 'pose' in any particular sense.

Carson: It is a favourite word of your own.

Wilde: Is it? I have no pose in this matter. In writing a play or book I am concerned entirely with literature; that is, with art. I aim not at doing good or evil, but in trying to make a thing that will have some quality or form of beauty or wit.

Carson: This is in your introduction to *Dorian Gray:* 'There is no such thing as a moral or an immoral book. Books are well written or badly written. That is all.' That expresses your view?

Wilde: My view on art, yes.

Carson: Then I take it that no matter how immoral a book may be, if it is well written it is, in your opinion, a good book?

Wilde: Yes: if it were well written so as to produce a sense of beauty, which is the highest sense of which a human being can be capable. If it were badly written it would produce a sense of disgust.

Carson: Then a well-written book putting forward perverted moral views may be a good book?

Wilde: No work of art ever puts forward views. Views belong to people who are not artists.

Wilde once remarked that what really amused him was to entertain the working classes, to enrage the middle-classes, and to fascinate the aristocracy. He was probably more successful in the second of these ambitions than in the other two, though he was certainly lionised and made much of in many aristocratic houses. But in February 1891, there appeared under his name in *The Fortnightly Review* a long essay entitled 'The Soul of Man under Socialism'. This essay antagonised many of his noble friends, to whom anything smacking of Socialism was anathema, and was looked upon in very much the same way as Communism is regarded today. What Oscar really advocated was the raising of the standard of living of the workers, not so much by giving them better living conditions, but by educating them through the arts; if barbarians could be persuaded to take an interest in the arts, they would cease to be barbarians. He admitted that there were difficulties in the way of his Utopian reforms, but that was not his concern; let others work out the details. He wrote, 'It will, of course, be said that such a scheme as is set forth here is quite unpractical, and goes against human nature. This is why it is worth carrying out, and that is why one proposes it.' There is no doubt that this essay annoyed the ruling classes of the day, who were quite prepared to let things go on as they were, so

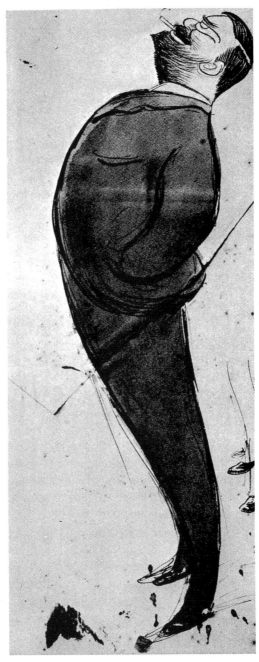

A caricature of the painter J. S. Sargent by Max Beerbohm

Wilde's second book of fairy-tales, 1891.
The first book, *The Happy Prince*, had
appeared in 1888

long as their own comfortable way of life was not disturbed. They still tolerated Wilde for his wit, but they never really forgave him, and when disaster overcame him, they shook wise heads, as though to say: 'I told you so!'

'A House of Pomegranates'

Mention has already been made of Oscar Wilde's second book of 'fairy-tales', *A House of Pomegranates*, which appeared towards the end of 1891. This contained four stories: 'The Young King', 'The Birthday of the Infanta', 'The Fisherman and His Soul', and 'The Star-Child'. It was intended to be one of the most beautifully produced books of the century. The decorative design of it was confided to Charles Ricketts and the illustrations were by C. H. Shannon; both these artists subsequently became Royal Academicians. Unfortunately, however, for the success of the scheme, the paper chosen for the book was unsuitable for Shannon's delicate drawings, which, in reproduction, appeared rather faint and nebulous.

The stories, however, enchanted everyone, though the newspapers were quite

Algernon Charles Swinburne,
a visitor to Tite Street

mystified as to how anyone who had written *Dorian Gray* could write such beautiful tales. They also thought that there must be a conventional connection between fairy-tales and children and complained that children would not be able to understand them; they could not grasp the fact that a fairy-tale might be written for 'grown-ups'. The reviewer of the *Pall Mall Gazette* seemed to be suffering under this delusion and drew forth the following letter from Wilde:

'To the Editor of the *Pall Mall Gazette*.

'Sir,—I have just had sent to me from London a copy of the *Pall Mall Gazette* containing a review of my book *A House of Pomegranates*. The writer of this review makes a certain suggestion which I beg you will allow me to correct.

'He starts by asking an extremely silly question, and that is whether or not I have written this book for the purpose of giving pleasure to the British child. Having expressed grave doubts on this subject, a subject on which I cannot

Walt Whitman, whose work Wilde discussed

Walter Crane, who illustrated *The Happy Prince*

conceive any fairly educated person having any doubts at all, he proceeds, apparently quite seriously, to make the extremely limited vocabulary at the disposal of the British child the standard by which the prose of an artist is to be judged! Now, in building this *House of Pomegranates,* I had about as much intention of pleasing the British child as I had of pleasing the British public. Mamillius is as entirely delightful as Caliban is entirely detestable, but neither the standard of Mamillius nor the standard of Caliban is my standard. No artist recognises any standard of beauty but that which is suggested by his own temperament. The artist seeks to realise, in a certain material, his immaterial idea of beauty, and thus to transform an idea into an ideal. That is the way an artist makes things. That is why an artist makes things. The artist has no other object in making things. Does your reviewer imagine that Mr Shannon, for instance, whose delicate and lovely illustrations he confesses himself quite unable to see, draws for the purpose of giving information to the blind?

'I remain, Sir, your obedient servant,

'OSCAR WILDE.'

ST. JAMES'S THEATRE,

Sole Lessee and Manager · · Mr. GEORGE ALEXANDER.

On Saturday, February 20th, 1892, at 8.30 punctually, and Every Evening,
A New and Original Play, in Four Acts, by OSCAR WILDE, entitled

Lady Windermere's Fan

Lord Windermere	Mr. GEORGE ALEXANDER
Lord Darlington	... Mr. NUTCOMBE GOULD
Lord Augustus Lorton	... Mr. H. H. VINCENT
Mr. Charles Dumby	... Mr. A. VANE TEMPEST
Mr. Cecil Graham	... Mr. BEN WEBSTER
Mr. Hopper	Mr. ALFRED HOLLES
Parker	... Mr. V. SANSBURY
Lady Windermere	Miss LILY HANBURY
The Duchess of Berwick	Miss FANNY COLEMAN
Lady Plimdale	Miss GRANVILLE
Mrs. Cowper-Cowper	... Miss A. DE WINTON
Lady Jedburgh	Miss B. PAGE
Lady Agatha Carlisle	Miss LAURA GRAVES
Rosalie	... Miss W. DOLAN
Mrs. Erlynne	Miss MARION TERRY

ACTS I & IV.	Morning-Room at Lord Windermere's, Carlton House Terrace	(H. P. Hall)
ACT II.	Drawing-Room at Lord Windermere's	(Walter Hann)
ACT III.	Lord Darlington's Rooms.	(W. Harford)

The Incidental Music by WALTER SLAUGHTER. The Furniture and Draperies by Messrs. FRANK GILES & Co., Kensington. The Dresses by Mesdames SAVAGE and PURDUE. The Wigs by Mr. C. H. FOX. The Etchings and Engravings in the corridors and vestibule kindly lent by Mr. I. P. MENDOZA, King Street, St. James's.

PROGRAMME OF MUSIC.

OVERTURE...	... "Marco Spado"	... ... Auber	WALTZ	... "Papillons Bleus"	... ...	Waldteufel
NEW BALLAD...	... "Stall "	... Walter Slaughter	OVERTURE	... "Il Seraglio " ...	... ...	Mozart
OVERTURE...	... "Le Caid" ...	... Ambrose Thomas		" Toreador and Andalouse "...	...	Rubenstein

Wilde's first successful play

Possibly the best of these stories is 'The Fisherman and His Soul'. The young fisherman catches a Mermaid, the only daughter of the Sea-King, in his net.

'So beautiful was she that when the young fisherman saw her he was filled with wonder, he put out his hand and drew the net close to him and, leaning over the side, he clasped her in his arms. . . . Her hair was as a wet fleece of gold, and each separate hair as a thread of fine gold in a cup of glass. Her body was as white ivory, and her tail was of silver and pearl. Silver and pearl was her tail, and the green weeds of the sea coiled round it, and like sea-shells were her ears, and her lips were like sea-coral.'

The young fisherman falls in love with the little mermaid; but as it is a mortal sin for a human to love one of the sea-folk, his soul chided him for his sin and so great was his love for the little mermaid that he drove his soul away from him. And one day, as he sat by the shore, gazing out over the sea and dreaming of his love, her dead body was washed ashore by the waves. And 'he kissed with mad lips the cold lips of the mermaid, and his heart within him brake. And as

The dramatic climax in Act II of *Lady Windermere's Fan*

through the fullness of his love his heart did break, the soul found an entrance and entered in, and was one with him even as before.'

Three months after the publication of *A House of Pomegranates,* in February 1892, Oscar embarked upon the succession of triumphs that were to be his for the next three years, with the production of his first successful play, *Lady Windermere's Fan,* at the St James's Theatre, with George Alexander as Lord Windermere, Lily Hanbury as Lady Windermere, and Marion Terry as Mrs Erlynne. The story of the play is, simply, that of a woman who ruins her own reputation in order to save that of the daughter who is unaware of the relationship between them. Oscar himself described it as 'one of those modern drawing-room plays with pink lampshades'. He had promised to write a play for Alexander early in the previous year but, as has been noted, he was kept very busy with other work, and he did not begin to write it seriously until late in the summer; so autumn was well on its way when he sent Alexander the text of *Lady Windermere's Fan.* Alexander, well known for his astuteness and business

'Lady Windermere's Fan'

80

George Alexander and Lily Hanbury   Nutcombe Gould and Marion Terry

acumen, tried to make the author sell the play to him outright for £1000. Wilde, however, knew enough of Alexander to suspect the motive behind the suggestion and replied: 'I have so much confidence in your excellent judgment, my dear Alec, that I cannot but refuse your generous offer.' How right he was in refusing is shown by the fact that he received £7000 in royalties from that first production alone.

The play had a tremendous reception by the fashionable audience which had gathered to see whether Wilde was as brilliant a playwright as he was a conversationalist. They were not disappointed; as epigram succeeded epigram and tense situations followed one another in rapid succession, the audience grew more and more enthusiastic and, when the curtain dropped on the last act, there were thunderous cries of 'Author!' Wilde strolled on to the stage with a lighted cigarette in his gloved hand, bowed and addressed the people present as follows: 'Ladies and Gentlemen. I have enjoyed this evening *immensely*. The actors have given us a charming rendering of a delightful play, and your appreciation has been most intelligent. I congratulate you on the great success of your performance, which persuades me that you think almost as highly of the play as I do.'

The audience was delighted by this short speech, but not so the critics, who were deeply shocked by Wilde appearing before the curtain smoking a cigarette. Clement Scott, the doyen of English critics, instead of criticising the play itself, concentrated on Oscar's bad manners in this respect, saying: 'People of birth and breeding don't do such things.' Most of the other critics damned the play with faint praise, irritated at being confronted with a new form of art which they did not really understand. But no adverse newspaper comment could prevent all London from flocking to see *Lady Windermere*. Lines from the play were quoted everywhere and were referred to on the music hall stage. There was even a *pastiche* of the play, called *The Poet and the Puppets*, written by James Glover and Charles Brookfield, the last named being, for some unexplained reason probably connected with jealousy, an implacable enemy of Wilde. This play was produced on 19th May at the Comedy Theatre in London, but was not a success.

'Salomé' When Oscar had finished writing *The Fan* in the previous autumn, he retired to Paris, where he wrote *Salomé*, his Biblical play in one act, which was again to bring him into the limelight. The actual circumstances of the writing of *Salomé* have always been the subject of argument, but the true facts are given in some unpublished recollections by Stuart Merrill, a Franco-American poet who was a friend of Wilde's. He says:

'*Salomé* was written in French by Wilde, then revised and corrected by me, Retté and Pierre Louÿs, in that order, but solely from the point of view of the language. Marcel Schwob corrected the proofs. Wilde was thus the sole author of *Salomé*, any corrections that were made being only for the purpose of drawing attention to the faults in his French.'

In any case the play was a real *tour de force*. Wilde was accused of anachronisms and plagiarism in writing it, but Robert Ross disposes of these accusations as follows:

'It has been remarked that Wilde confuses Herod the Great (Matt. ii, 1), Herod Antipas (Matt. xiv, 3) and Herod Agrippa (Acts xii. 1). But the confusion is intentional, as in medieval mystery plays Herod is taken for a type, not an historical character, and the criticism is about as valuable as that of people who laboriously point out the anachronisms in Beardsley's designs for the play. With reference to the charge of plagiarism brought against *Salomé* and its author, I venture to mention a personal recollection. Wilde complained to me one day that someone, in a well-known novel, had stolen an idea of his. I pleaded in

The proscenium of the St James's Theatre, rebuilt after fire.
The original theatre was the scene of all George Alexander's triumphs

A fifteenth-century representation of Salomé dancing before Herod

defence of the culprit that Wilde himself was a fearless literary thief. "My dear fellow," he said, with his usual drawling emphasis, "when I see a monstrous tulip with *four* wonderful petals in someone else's garden, I am impelled to grow a monstrous tulip with *five* wonderful petals; but that is no reason why someone should grow a tulip with only *three* petals."'

'Salomé' refused a licence

Salomé was not written, as it has been often asserted, for Sarah Bernhardt, but it was certainly submitted to her, as she put it into rehearsal at the Palace Theatre, London, with herself in the title-role, a year before it was published in book form. The Lord Chamberlain, however, refused a licence to the play under a rule, then in force, which forbade the representation of Biblical characters on the public stage in England. The text of the play was published in Paris in the following year, and an English translation (not, oddly enough, made by Wilde

'The Peacock Skirt', a decoration by Aubrey Beardsley for the English translation of *Salomé*, 1894

Beardsley's half title to the
English *Salomé*, 1894

himself) was published in London, with illustrations or, more accurately, decorations by Aubrey Beardsley, who was just beginning to become known as an artist of the macabre.

Wilde, with the success of *Lady Windermere's Fan* still ringing in his head, was furious about the Lord Chamberlain's attitude, though he must have known that there was grave risk of a licence being refused. The rule under which it was refused was one made at the time of the Reformation, with a view to the suppression of Catholic 'Mystery Plays', and Wilde ought to have known of it. Sarah Bernhardt, on the other hand, had no reason to know of the existence of such a rule, and was quite justifiably annoyed at having wasted so much time and money. Indignation made Wilde lose his sense of proportion, and without any thought of the reaction that such an announcement was bound to provoke, he declared his intention, in a Paris newspaper, of renouncing his British nationality and becoming a Frenchman, stating, 'My resolution is deliberately taken. Since it is impossible to have a work of art performed in England, I shall transfer myself to another fatherland, of which I have long been enamoured.' *Punch* could not let such an opportunity slip, and came out with a cartoon, by

Imaginary interview between Oscar Wilde and the Lord Chamberlain, who refused on religious grounds to grant a licence for the stage performance of *Salomé*

Bernard Partridge, representing Oscar in the uniform of a private soldier in the French army.

As matters turned out, it is a pity that Oscar did not carry out his threat to adopt French citizenship, but his natural buoyancy soon returned to him, and he forgave everyone concerned, including himself, for this temporary set-back, and was soon engaged upon another play, this time at the instigation of his old friend Herbert Beerbohm Tree. He did not write the play with Tree in view for any particular part. The only play he had written with any character in mind was *The Duchess of Padua* for Mary Anderson, and that venture was a failure. He once remarked to a friend of his, 'I never write plays for anyone. I write plays to amuse myself. Later, if anyone wants to act in them, I sometimes allow him to do so.' The play that he wrote this time, in the summer of 1892, was *A Woman of No Importance*.

'*A Woman of No Importance*'

The play was produced on 19th April 1893, at the Haymarket Theatre, London, with Tree and Mrs Bernard Beere in the principal parts of Lord Illingworth and Mrs Arbuthnot, and Julia Neilson and Fred Terry in the *jeune premier* parts of Hester Worsley and Gerald Arbuthnot. The plot is the only

A *Punch* cartoon: 'A Wilde Idea'

Caricature of Herbert Beerbohm Tree, by Harry Furniss

one of Wilde's chief plays which is definitely dated, in that, at the end it produces a situation which, owing to changes in the law, would ring false today. Mrs Arbuthnot refuses to marry Lord Illingworth, the father of her illegitimate child by him, because of her contempt for the father. Nowadays, however, by marrying Lord Illingworth she would have legitimised her son and made him heir to the title—a step which any fond mother would have considered it her duty to take. In spite of this, and because of the brilliant dialogue, the play continues to be revived from time to time.

A Woman of No Importance was an immediate success and was received enthusiastically by the first night audience, which, as in the case of *Lady Windermere's Fan,* rose to its feet and made the theatre ring with cries of 'Author!' Wilde, not wishing to repeat his mistake on the occasion of the first night of *The Fan,* rose to his own feet in the box which he was occupying with friends and announced: 'Ladies and gentlemen, I regret to inform you that Mr Oscar Wilde is not in the house.'

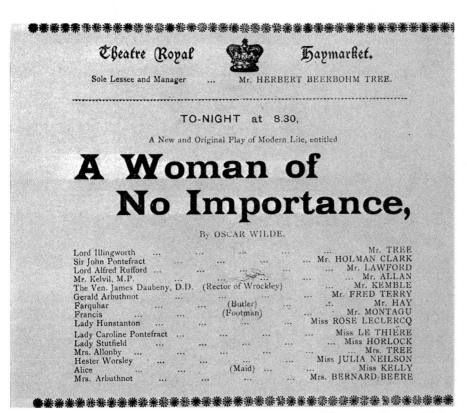

Theatre Royal ♔ Haymarket.

Sole Lessee and Manager ... Mr. HERBERT BEERBOHM TREE.

TO-NIGHT at 8.30,

A New and Original Play of Modern Life, entitled

A Woman of No Importance,

By OSCAR WILDE.

Lord Illingworth	... Mr. TREE
Sir John Pontefract	... Mr. HOLMAN CLARK
Lord Alfred Rufford	... Mr. LAWFORD
Mr. Kelvil, M.P.	... Mr. ALLAN
The Ven. James Daubeny, D.D. (Rector of Wrockley)	... Mr. KEMBLE
Gerald Arbuthnot	... Mr. FRED TERRY
Farquhar (Butler) ...	... Mr. HAY
Francis ... ... (Footman)	... Mr. MONTAGU
Lady Hunstanton	Miss ROSE LECLERCQ
Lady Caroline Pontefract	... Miss LE THIÈRE
Lady Stutfield	... Miss HORLOCK
Mrs. Allonby	... Mrs. TREE
Hester Worsley	Miss JULIA NEILSON
Alice ... ... (Maid) ...	... Miss KELLY
Mrs. Arbuthnot	Mrs. BERNARD-BEERE

Wilde's second successful play

The critics had been annoyed in the earlier play by action being held up while the characters delivered themselves of strings of paradoxes and epigrams, and they complained of the same lack of action now. Oscar's reply was, 'I wrote the first act of *A Woman of No Importance* in answer to the critics who said that *Lady Windermere's Fan* lacked action. In the act in question there was absolutely no action at all. It was a perfect act.' Nevertheless, the critics were far more tolerant of this play than they had been of the previous one. They had by this time realised that antagonism to a Wilde play could not dissuade the public from going to see it, and they did not want theatre-goers to disregard their advice entirely. They may even have been told by their editors to modify their resentment and bitterness against these new departures from convention and tradition, and particularly against an author who showed by his utterances and his demeanour that he cared nothing at all for them or for their abuse.

Oscar's reputation as a wit and a conversationalist could not help travelling across the Channel, where French literary and artistic circles prided themselves

The scene just before the curtain of the Second Act of *A Woman of No Importance*

on those same qualities. He naturally took advantage of this and spent a great deal of his time in Paris, where he was fêted even more than he was in England. His actions and sayings were reported almost daily in the Paris Press. Typical of those visits was his meeting with Yvette Guilbert, the well-known French singer and *diseuse*. 'Monsieur Wilde,' she said to him on being introduced, 'en moi vous voyez la femme la plus laide de Paris!' Many people would have protested and floundered over a stout denial, but Oscar, realising how pleased she was with her claim, bowed deeply and replied: 'Au contraire. Du monde, madame, du monde!'

'*The Sphinx*' After the production of *A Woman of No Importance* in April 1893, nothing of Wilde's, except a few articles, appeared until June, when his poem *The Sphinx* was published. This was an even more elaborately produced book than *A House of Pomegranates* had aspired to be, and was one of the most elegant of the many beautiful books for which John Lane, of the Bodley Head publishing house, was responsible in the 1890s. It was printed in different coloured inks on

A French caricature of Oscar Wilde

Paris in the Nineties

rather rough hand-made paper and bound in white vellum with a gilt design by Charles Ricketts, who also decorated the verses and illustrated them.

Oscar conceived the idea of the poem in his Oxford days and started writing it seriously in Paris on his return from his first American visit, working at it spasmodically for the next eight years. All kinds of sinister meanings were read into the poem—perversity, decadence, sensuality, in fact anything the particular reader or critic happened to dislike. But it is really nothing more deadly than an experiment at playing with words. Words, to Oscar Wilde, were beautiful baubles with which to play and build, as a child plays with coloured bricks. Over a period of years he collected and stored up words for this poem—the names of mythical beasts and birds and of rare and precious stones, and words describing strange sensations; and to the really prudish mind sensation is nearly always synonymous with vice. He delighted in finding almost impossible rhymes for peculiar words—'pedestalled' to rhyme with 'emerald', 'hieroglyph' with 'hippogriff', 'catafalque' with 'Amenalk'.

Lord Alfred Bruce Douglas, third son of
the eighth Marquess of Queensberry

The metre of *The Sphinx* is the same as that of Tennyson's *In Memoriam*, but it is not, by reason of that, a plagiarism. When some pedant pointed this similarity out to Oscar, he replied: 'Yes, but it is printed quite differently.' This has often been quoted as a humorous remark; but Wilde did not mean it to be so; it happened to be true; Tennyson's poem was printed in stanzas of four lines; Wilde's was printed in couplets.

Although Oscar travelled about and dawdled a great deal during the year 1894, it was in this year that he wrote his last two plays, *An Ideal Husband* and *The Importance of Being Earnest*. Little did he guess at that time what relentless fate had in store for him, though he might have taken a warning from the behaviour of the eighth Marquess of Queensberry, who was going about London abusing him and threatening to disgrace and ruin him; the cause of this was the friendship that had sprung up between Oscar Wilde and the Marquess's youngest son, Lord Alfred Bruce Douglas.

Lord Alfred Douglas

One day in 1891 a young poet named Lionel Pigot Johnson, himself only twenty-four years of age, brought an Oxford undergraduate round to Tite Street to see Oscar; the young man was Lord Alfred Douglas, the spoilt darling of his mother and a constant source of irritation to his father. This father was a despot and a bully in his own house; his wife and his children were terrified of him and pandered slavishly to him, all except Alfred, who was in the habit of defying him and ridiculing him to his face. This attitude so infuriated the Marquess that he conceived a bitter hatred for his son, and determined to go to any lengths to shame and disgrace him.

Lord Queensberry's attack

Oscar Wilde immediately took a liking to the young man and a close friendship sprang up between the two. This, coming to Queensberry's ears, gave him the opportunity for which he was seeking. Oscar's aestheticism and preciosity had already given rise to certain rumours, and Queensberry added fuel to the fire

THE SPHINX BY OSCAR WILDE

MELAN CHOLIA

WITH DECORATIONS BY CHARLES RICKETTS
LONDON MDCCCXCIV
ELKIN MATHEWS AND JOHN LANE . AT THE SIGN OF THE BODLEY HEAD.
BOSTON
COPELAND AND DAY LXIX CORNHILL

Title-page of Wilde's fantasy *The Sphinx*, designed by Charles Ricketts

A page from one of the drafts of *The Sphinx*, with a humorous sketch of a schoolmaster chasing children, by Oscar Wilde himself

by proclaiming to all who would listen to him that his beloved son was being debauched by the inhuman monster Oscar Wilde. There is no doubt that Oscar was devoted to Alfred Douglas, but the attraction was mainly caused by four qualities that Alfred possessed: he was a member of a very old and aristocratic family, he had youth, he was exceptionally good-looking and, although only twenty-one, was already showing great promise as a poet, particularly as a writer of sonnets, which was the form of poetry that appealed most to Oscar.

Matters came to a head with the Marquess forcing his way into Oscar's house in Tite Street and repeating his accusations of unnatural practices. The interview, however, did not quite turn out as the Marquess had hoped, and he was forced to beat an ignominious retreat, accompanied by the ex-prize-fighter whom he had brought with him to lend him physical support.

Wilde refused to be intimidated by Queensberry and continued his friendship with Alfred Douglas. He refused, also, to see the danger in which he stood;

Theatre Royal — Haymarket.

Sole Lessee	Mr. TREE.
Managers ...	Mr. LEWIS WALLER AND Mr. H. H. MORELL.

Mr. TREE begs to announce that during his absence in America his Theatre has been taken for the Spring Season by Mr. LEWIS WALLER and Mr. H. H. MORELL.

LAST NIGHTS of "An Ideal Husband," in consequence of the approaching termination of Messrs. WALLER & MORELL's tenancy of this Theatre.

EXTENDED RUN.—Arrangements have been made with Mr. Tree whereby the run of "AN IDEAL HUSBAND" at this Theatre will be prolonged until Saturday, April 6th. On Thursday, March 28th, will take place the **100TH** performance of "AN IDEAL HUSBAND."

TO-NIGHT at 8.30, A New and Original Play of Modern Life, entitled

AN IDEAL HUSBAND,

By OSCAR WILDE.

The Earl of Caversham, K.G.	Mr. ALFRED BISHOP
Lord Goring ... (his Son) ...	Mr. CHARLES H. HAWTREY
Sir Robert Chiltern	Mr. LEWIS WALLER
(Under Secretary for Foreign Affairs)	
Vicomte de Nanjac	Mr. COSMO STUART
Mr. Montford	Mr. HENRY STANFORD
Phipps	Mr. CHARLES BROOKFIELD
Mason	Mr. H. DEANE
Footman ... ... (at Lord Goring's) ...	Mr. CHARLES MEYRICK
Footman ... (at Sir Robert Chiltern's) ...	Mr. GOODHART
Lady Chiltern	Miss JULIA NEILSON
Lady Markby	Miss FANNY BROUGH
Lady Basildon	Miss VANE FEATHERSTON
Mrs. Marchmont	Miss HELEN FORSYTH
Miss Mabel Chiltern ... (Sir Robert's Sister)	Miss MAUDE MILLETT
Mrs. Cheveley	Miss FLORENCE WEST

Wilde's third successful play

perhaps success had gone to his head and he considered that accepted standards of conduct were not for him, and that he was, as it were, above the law. Meanwhile, that success continued.

On 3rd January 1895, Oscar Wilde's third important play, *An Ideal Husband*, was produced by Lewis Waller and H. H. Morell at the Haymarket Theatre, London. It was an immediate success, both from a financial and a social point of view. The Prince of Wales, who already knew and liked Oscar, was present in a box at the first night; then, as now, it was very rare for royalty to be seen at a theatre on the first night of a play. He warmly congratulated the author, and his approval brought the critics to heel and the play-going public to the theatre. The play, though not so dramatic as the previous two plays, was better constructed and showed that Oscar was getting a firmer grip of the technique of the theatre. There was, as usual, a great deal of paradox, epigram, and what can only be described as 'serious nonsense' in the play. Perhaps the most

'An Ideal Husband'

Lewis Waller and Julia Neilson in one
of the tense scenes from *An Ideal Husband*

interesting contemporary comment on *An Ideal Husband* was the one by Bernard
Shaw in the *Saturday Review* :

'Mr Oscar Wilde's new play at the Haymarket is a dangerous subject, because
he has the property of making his critics dull. They laugh angrily at his epigrams,
like a child who is coaxed into being amused in the very act of setting up a yell
of rage and agony. They protest that the trick is obvious, and that such epigrams
can be turned out by the score by anyone light-minded enough to condescend
to such frivolity. As far as I can ascertain, I am the only person in London who
cannot sit down and write an Oscar Wilde play at will. The fact that his plays,
though apparently lucrative, remain unique under these circumstances, says
much for the self-denial of our scribes. In a certain sense Mr Wilde is to me our
only thorough playwright. He plays with everything: with wit, with philosophy,
with drama, with actors and audience, with the whole theatre.'

Shaw went on to say that the three best epigrams in *An Ideal Husband* would
for ever remain secrets between Mr Wilde and a few chosen spirits. All that the

George Bernard Shaw as a young man

public asked for in those days was diversion; they were tired of their own seriousness; they delighted in the frivolity with which that impertinent Irishman attacked every citadel of English convention, and they did not mind being laughed at because they felt quite immune to outside criticism of any kind.

Wilde pretended, as usual, not to be in the least interested in how the dramatic critics received his play and voiced his opinion of such gentlemen in a long interview with him that appeared in *The Sketch*. Among his replies to the interviewer we read:

'For a man to be a dramatic critic is as foolish and inartistic as it would be for a man to be a critic of epics or a pastoral critic or a critic of lyrics.' 'The moment criticism exercises any influence, it ceases to be criticism. The aim of the true critic is to try to chronicle his own moods, not to try to correct the masterpieces of others.' 'I never reply to my critics. I have far too much time. But I think some day I will give a general answer in the form of a lecture, which I shall call "Straight Talks to Old Men".'

ST. JAMES'S THEATRE.

SOLE LESSEE AND PROPRIETOR - - MR. GEORGE ALEXANDER.

PRODUCED THURSDAY, FEBRUARY 14th, 1895.

To-day at 3, and Every Evening at 9,

The Importance of being Earnest,

A TRIVIAL COMEDY FOR SERIOUS PEOPLE.

John Worthing, J.P.	of the Manor House, Woolton, Hertfordshire	Mr. GEORGE ALEXANDER
Algernon Moncrieffe	(his Friend)	Mr. ALLAN AYNESWORTH
Rev. Canon Chasuble, D.D.	(Rector of Woolton)	Mr. H. H. VINCENT
Merriman	(Butler to Mr. Worthing)	Mr. FRANK DYALL
Lane	(Mr. Moncrieffe's Man-servant)	Mr. F. KINSEY PEILE
Lady Bracknell		Mrs. EDWARD SAKER
Hon. Gwendolen Fairfax	(her Daughter)	Miss IRENE VANBRUGH
Cecily Cardew	(John Worthing's Ward)	Miss VIOLET LYSTER
Miss Prism	(her Governess)	Mrs GEORGE CANNINGE

Time - - The Present.

Act I. - Algernon Moncrieffe's Rooms in Piccadilly (*H. P. Hall*)
Act II. - The Garden at the Manor House, Woolton (*H. P. Hall*)
Act III. - Morning-Room at the Manor House, Woolton (*Walter Hann*)

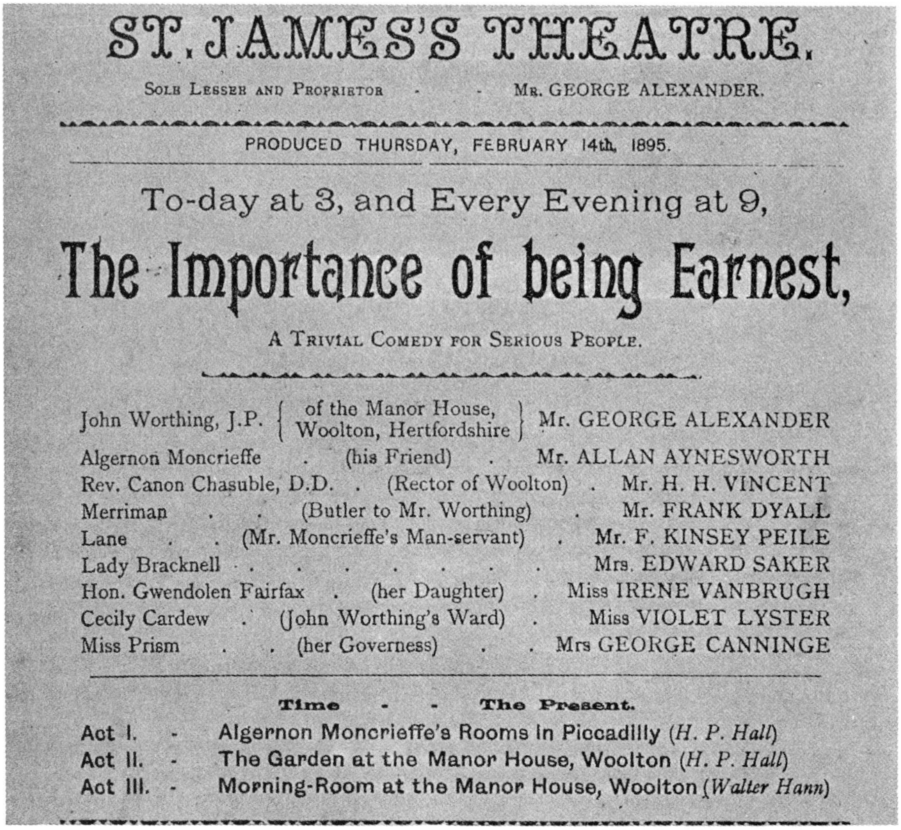

Wilde's fourth and last successful play

'The Importance of Being Earnest'

The next, last, and most important of Oscar's plays, the idea of which had first occurred to him earlier in the year, was written in September by the seaside where he had taken a house and lived a life of domesticity with his wife and children. This was *The Importance of Being Earnest*. He was very anxious that George Alexander should play the leading part of John Worthing; so, with admirable insight into Alexander's character, he submitted the play to him, accompanied by a letter of which the following is an extract:

'As you wish to see my somewhat farcical comedy, I send you the first copy of it. It is called *Lady Lancing* on the cover, but the real title is *The Importance of Being Earnest*. Of course the play is not suitable to you at all: you are a romantic actor: the people it wants are actors like Wyndham and Hawtrey. Also, I would be sorry if you altered the artistic line of progress you have always

George Alexander and Allan Aynesworth, two men about town in *The Importance of Being Ernest*

followed at the St James's; but of course read it, and let me know what you think about it.'

This was a challenge that no actor, least of all George Alexander, could possibly resist, as no actor worthy of the name would ever admit that there was any part in any play that he was unable to interpret. So Alexander replied that he was enchanted with the play and would like to produce it, with himself in one of the two leading male parts—the one which Wilde wanted him to play, that of John Worthing. The other leading man was Allan Aynesworth, in the part of Algernon Moncrieff. Of the ladies, Rose Leclerq played Lady Bracknell, Irene Vanbrugh took the part of Gwendolen Fairfax, and Evelyn Millard that of Cecily Cardew.

As originally written, *The Importance of Being Earnest* was a four-act play; but

Charles Hawtrey, who played the part of
Lord Goring in *An Ideal Husband*

Alexander, wishing to provide a 'curtain raiser', as was usual in those days, asked Oscar to reduce it to three acts. This was done, and it is the three-act version that has been played ever since, though the four-act version is still in existence and was published in a separate book by Methuen & Co in 1957. There is no doubt that the three-act version was an improvement on the four-act original, though the exclusion of Mr Gribsby, a solicitors' clerk who came down to the country to serve a writ of attachment on the mythical Ernest Worthing seems a pity, as his appearance was only a very short one and affected a great deal of the subsequent dialogue of the play.

*Lord Queensberry's
renewed attack*

Oscar Wilde and Alfred Douglas went on holiday to Algiers while the play was being rehearsed; and Queensberry, finding out about this, flew into a renewed state of fury and determined to try to wreck Oscar's new play. He accordingly booked a seat for the first night of *The Importance,* with the object of making a scene there. This came to the ears of Alexander, who had the booking cancelled and gave orders that the Marquess was not to be admitted to any part of the house, stationing guards at all the entrances to see that his orders were carried out. Queensberry was not, however, to be so easily deterred, and turned up with a 'bouquet' of carrots and turnips, which he intended to throw on the stage if the author was called for at the end of the performance. He was foiled in this intention and finally left, after leaving his 'bouquet' at the stage door.

Irene Vanbrugh as Gwendolen Fairfax in *The Importance of Being Ernest*

The Importance of Being Earnest was produced at the St James's Theatre on the evening of 14th February 1895, and was received with rapturous delight by both audience and critics. With this play Wilde had conquered London after a long and, at times, very uphill struggle. He had now reached the pinnacle of his success. *The Importance* at the St James's Theatre, *An Ideal Husband* at the Haymarket, London, and at the Lyceum in New York, were all drawing crowded and enthusiastic audiences, and actor-managers everywhere were besieging him with entreaties to write plays for them. He had, indeed, several plots for plays running in his head, but suddenly something happened that put all thought of work out of his mind for the time being.

The Marquess of Queensberry, foiled in his attempt to create a disturbance at the St James's Theatre, and infuriated by the unanimous praise heaped on the play by the critics, tried a new line of attack. Four days after the first night, on 18th February, he drove with a witness to the Albemarle Club in Dover Street, of which Oscar was a member, and left his card with the Hall Porter to be handed to Oscar. On the card he wrote the words: 'To Oscar Wilde, posing as a somdomite [sic].' It transpired later that the offending word, whether because of its mis-spelling, or because he was unfamiliar with it, did not convey any meaning to the Hall Porter; the circumstances were, however, so unusual, that he put it in an envelope, addressed it 'Oscar Wilde, Esq.' and stuck it in the letter-rack in the hall. And it was there that Oscar received it ten days later, on his return from visiting friends in the country. Here it was that he made the fatal mistake that ruined him. He should have torn up the card, dismissed the incident from his mind and let Queensberry brood on in his fury. Instead of doing this, he took the matter much too seriously and sent a note to his great friend Robert Ross, enclosing Queensberry's card, and asking him to come to see him; the note still exists:

'Since I saw you, something has happened. Bosie's father ["Bosie" was Lord Alfred Douglas's nickname] has left a card at my club with hideous words on it. I don't see anything now but a criminal prosecution. My whole life seems ruined by this man. The tower of ivory is assailed by the foul thing. On the sand is my life spilt.'

Arrest of Lord Queensberry

This was on 28th February. On 1st March, discouraged by his real friends, but egged on by Alfred Douglas, who had but one thought in his mind, namely to see his father in the dock, Wilde applied for a warrant for the arrest of the Marquess, who appeared on a charge of criminal libel at Marlborough Street Police Court on the following day. The case was adjourned for a week and, on Queensberry's reappearance at Marlborough Street, he was committed for trial at the Old Bailey, and released on £500 bail.

Robert Ross's solicitor, Charles Humphreys, who had been in charge of the proceedings up to this point, had now to give way to a member of the Bar, and he approached Sir Edward Clarke and asked him if he would lead for the prosecution. At that time Sir Edward was Solicitor-General in the Government, a position he had held for some years, and he had the reputation of never accepting a brief unless he was sure that his client had a good case and was in

Queensberry's card

The Marquess of Queensberry, an impression by Phil May in 1889

Oscar Wilde

the right. Sir Edward asked Humphreys to bring Wilde to his chambers and there he asked him point-blank whether there was any vestige of truth in the charge that Queensberry had brought against him; Wilde assured him that the charge was without any foundation. At that time the only evidence that Queensberry could bring in support of his accusation was contained in certain passages in *The Picture of Dorian Gray,* and Oscar's letters to Alfred Douglas, of which he had managed in some way to get possession. Had Wilde been more truthful, Sir Edward Clarke would undoubtedly have advised him to withdraw his prosecution, and to withdraw himself from the scene of conflict for a period.

The trial of the Marquess of Queensberry at the Old Bailey was not due to take place for another three weeks, so Wilde went to Monte Carlo with Alfred Douglas, as though he had not a care in the world. The Marquess, however,

Nice in the 1890s

spent the intervening time in concocting evidence, a great deal of it false, to bolster up his defence, and when Wilde returned to London shortly before the trial, he began to realise the seriousness of his position. He still thought, in spite of the evidence that he knew Queensberry had collected or manufactured that he would win the day.

Alas for human hopes! On 3rd April the case of Regina *v*. the Marquess of Queensberry was opened at the Old Bailey before Mr Justice Henn Collins and lasted three days, at the end of which Sir Edward Clarke, seeing the hopelessness of the position, withdrew from the case and a formal verdict of 'Not Guilty' was returned in Queensberry's favour. From that point the real *débâcle* began. Queensberry became the hero of the hour and on the evening of his acquittal Charles Brookfield and Charles Hawtrey, who had been, and still

Trial of Lord Queensberry

The first Judge, Mr Justice Henn Collins Sir Edward Clarke, Wilde's counsel in all three trials

were, acting in *An Ideal Husband,* gave him a supper-party to celebrate his triumph. These two actors had always hated and been jealous of Oscar, and now was their golden opportunity for grinding the object of their dislike into the mud.

In a last effort to defend himself, Oscar wrote a letter to the *Evening News :*

'It would have been impossible for me to have proved my case without putting Lord Alfred Douglas in the witness-box against his father. Lord Alfred Douglas was extremely anxious to go into the box, but I would not let him do so. Rather than put him into so painful a position, I decided to retire from the case, and to bear upon my own shoulders whatever ignominy and shame might result from my prosecution of Lord Queensberry.'

Oscar was urged by all his friends to go abroad and to let the turmoil subside. But he was dazed by the disaster that had befallen him and refused to go. He

Holloway Gaol, to which Wilde was sent after the failure of his action against Lord Queensberry

immediately went to the Cadogan Hotel in Sloane Street, where he had a room. Meanwhile, at the instigation of the solicitors acting for Lord Queensberry, the papers in the case that had just ended were sent to the Director of Public Prosecutions and no time was wasted. That evening the police called at the Cadogan Hotel and arrested Oscar Wilde. He was taken to Bow Street and formally charged under a section of the Criminal Law Amendment Act of 1885 and put into a cell. Next day he was taken in a Black Maria to Holloway Gaol, nowadays a prison for women, but in those days the prison to which all male prisoners were taken to await trial, if not granted bail. Oscar was not granted bail, which might have given him, in freedom, a chance to prepare his defence, or at any rate to show how much the evidence against him had been fabricated. It afterwards became quite clear that most of the witnesses against Oscar had been offered the alternatives of prison or perjury, and that they, wisely from their own point of view, had chosen perjury.

Wilde arrested

As an instance of the feeling against Wilde during the trials, this picture of a prehistoric monster was sent to him anonymously

Wilde's first trial   Three weeks elapsed between Wilde's arrest and his trial at the Old Bailey, where he stood in the same dock into which he had placed Lord Queensberry only a short time before. During those three weeks he was declared a bankrupt, the petitioner being Queensberry in respect of the costs of the case against him, and the contents of Wilde's house in Tite Street were sold by public auction.

Oscar's trial started on 26th April and lasted five days, at the end of which the jury disagreed and a verdict of 'Not Guilty' was returned on certain counts. So the whole wretched business had to be gone through again, about three weeks later. Although again refused bail at first, it was later granted, and Oscar Wilde spent the intervening period at the house of his friends Mr and Mrs Ernest Leverson, never leaving the house until after dark.

As an indication of the Marquess of Queensberry's violent nature and of the antipathy that existed between him and his family (his wife had divorced him eighteen years before when he suggested that his mistress should come to live with them), it is interesting to note that Lord Douglas of Hawick, the eldest son of the Marquess and Lord Alfred Douglas's brother, went surety for £1800 of

The judge at the last trial, Mr Justice Wills, who sentenced Wilde to two years' imprisonment with hard labour

the £5000 bail on which Oscar was released. And between the two trials Queensberry had a stand-up fight in St James's Street with his other son, Lord Percy Douglas, an incident that led them both to be charged with disorderly conduct in the Police Court next day.

The second trial started on 20th May 1895 at the Old Bailey before Mr Justice Wills and a jury of twelve men. It was a dreary repetition of the first trial and dragged on for six days. The judge was obviously against Oscar from the very start and he summed up dead against him. The jury brought in a verdict of guilty, and the learned judge addressed Oscar Wilde with such venom as has seldom been heard in a British Court of Law:

Wilde's second trial

'... It is no use for me to address you. People who can do these things must be dead to all sense of shame.... I shall be expected to pass the severest sentence that the law allows. In my judgment it is totally inadequate for such a case as this. The sentence of the Court is that you be imprisoned and kept to hard labour for two years.'

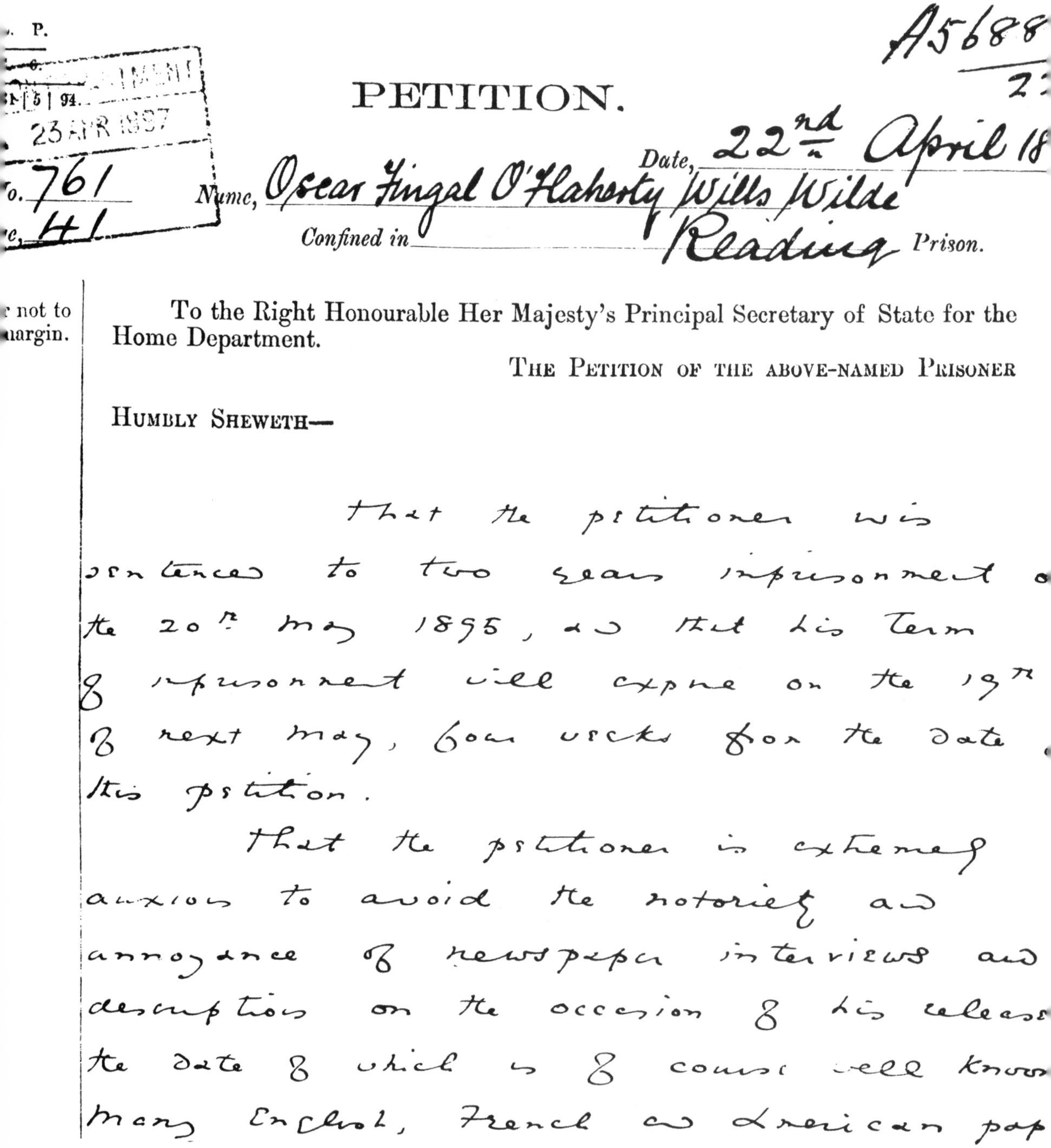

. P.

23 APR 1897

o. 761

c. 41

r not to
margin.

PETITION.

A5688

2.

Name, *Oscar Fingal O'Flaherty Wills Wilde* Date, 22nd April 18

Confined in *Reading* Prison.

To the Right Honourable Her Majesty's Principal Secretary of State for the Home Department.

THE PETITION OF THE ABOVE-NAMED PRISONER

HUMBLY SHEWETH—

that the petitioner was sentenced to two years imprisonment on the 20th May 1895, and that his Term of imprisonment will expire on the 19th of next May, four weeks from the date of this petition.

That the petitioner is extremely anxious to avoid the notoriety and annoyance of newspaper interviews and descriptions on the occasion of his release the date of which is of course well known to many English, French and American pap

The first page of one of Wilde's petitions for his release from prison. It was ignored

A woodcut by Frans Masereel for
The Ballad of Reading Gaol

And so began the martyrdom of Oscar Wilde. The maxim that the higher you climb the further you have to fall was seldom so true as it was in his case. The mental torture that he must have suffered is indescribable, as he was bereft of everything that made life bearable to him. Not only the material pleasures of life, but the society of his wife and children, the companionship of conversation, and above all books and writing materials were denied him. From Reading Gaol, where he spent most of his imprisonment, he addressed three petitions praying to have his sentence reduced, but they met with no response except that towards the end he was allowed pen and ink and paper. He was supplied with one sheet of blue folio prison paper, stamped with the Royal Arms, at a time. When this was filled, it was removed and replaced by another; and it was on these sheets that he wrote the long letter to Alfred Douglas which is now known as *De Profundis,* and which was the last prose work that he ever produced.

To use Oscar Wilde's own words, in *De Profundis* he tried to explain his conduct without defending it; he pinned the major blame for his downfall on Alfred Douglas himself, in a damning indictment which contains much scorn and bitterness. But it is also an Apologia and a General Confession. About half-way through the letter he writes:

'The gods had given me almost everything. I had genius, a distinguished name, high social position, brilliancy, intellectual daring; I made art a philosophy and philosophy an art; I altered the minds of men and the colours of things: there was nothing I said or did that did not make people wonder: I took

H. M. Prison.
Reading.

Dear Bosie,

After long and fruitless waiting I have determined to write to you myself, as much for your sake as for mine, as I would not like to think that I had passed through two long years of imprisonment without ever having received a single line from you, or any news or message even, except such as gave me pain.

Our ill-fated and most lamentable friendship has ended in ruin and public infamy for me, yet the memory of our ancient affection is often with me, and the thought that loathing, bitterness and contempt should for ever take that place in my heart once held by love is very sad to me: and you yourself will, I think, feel in your heart that to write to me as I lie in the loneliness of prison-life is better than to publish my letters without my permission or to dedicate poems to me unasked, though the world will know nothing of whatever words of grief or passion, of remorse or indifference you may choose to send as your answer or your appeal.

I have no doubt that in this letter in which I have to write of your life and of mine, of the past and of the future, of sweet things changed to bitterness and of bitter things that may be turned into joy, there will be much that will wound your vanity to the quick. If it prove so, read the letter over and over again till it kills your vanity. If you find in it something of which you feel that you are unjustly accused, remember that one should be thankful that there is any fault of which one can be unjustly accused. If there be in it one single passage that brings tears to your eyes, weep as we weep in prison where the day no less than the night is set apart for tears. It is the only thing that can save you. If you go complaining to your mother, as you did with reference to the scorn of you I displayed in my letter to Robbie, so that she may flatter and soothe you back into self-complacency or conceit, you will be completely lost. If you find one false excuse for yourself, you will soon find a hundred, and be just what you were before. Do you still say, as you said to Robbie in your answer, that I "attribute unworthy motives" to you? Ah! you had no motives in life. You had appetites merely. A motive is an intellectual aim. That you were "very young" when our friendship began? your defect was not that you knew so little about life, but that you knew so much. The morning dawn of boyhood with its delicate bloom, its clear pure light, its joy of innocence and expectation you had left far behind. With very swift and running feet you had passed from Romance to

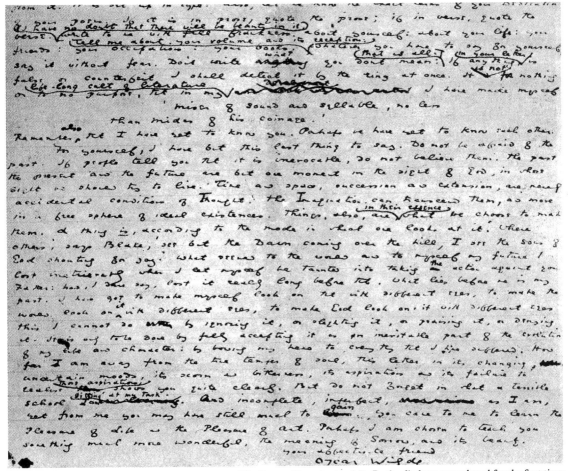

The first and last sheets of *De Profundis*, here reproduced for the first time

the drama, the most objective form known to art, and made it as personal a
mode of expression as the lyric or the sonnet, at the same time that I widened
its range and enriched its characterisation: drama, novel, poem in rhyme, poem
in prose, subtle or fantastic dialogue, whatever I touched I made beautiful in
a new mode of beauty: to truth itself I gave what is false no less than what is
true as its rightful province, and showed that the false and the true are merely
forms of intellectual existence. I treated art as the supreme reality, and life as a
mere mode of fiction: I awoke the imagination of my century so that it created
myth and legend around me: I summed up all systems in a phrase, and all
existence in an epigram. Along with these things, I had things that were
different. I let myself be lured into long spells of senseless and sensual ease. I
amused myself with being a *flâneur*, a dandy, a man of fashion. I surrounded

The title-page of the first publication of part of *De Profundis*. It was published in a German translation some months before the English edition

myself with the smaller natures and the meaner minds. I became the spendthrift of my own genius, and to waste an eternal youth gave me a curious joy. Tired of being on the heights I deliberately went to the depths in the search for new sensations. What the paradox was to me in the sphere of thought, perversity became to me in the sphere of passion. Desire, at the end, was a malady, or a madness, or both. I grew careless of the lives of others. I took pleasure where it pleased me and passed on. I forgot that every little action of the common day makes or unmakes character, and that therefore what one has done in the secret chamber one has someday to cry aloud on the housetop. I ceased to be Lord over myself. I was no longer the Captain of my Soul, and did not know it. I allowed you to dominate me, and your father to frighten me. I ended in horrible disgrace. There is only one thing for me now—absolute Humility: just as there is only one thing for you, absolute Humility also. You had better come down into the dust and learn it beside me.'

The frontispiece by Frans Masereel for *The Ballad of Reading Gaol*

De Profundis also contains some of the best of Oscar Wilde's mystical writings. Writing of the life of Christ and of the miracles recorded in the Bible, he says:

'His miracles seem to me as exquisite as the coming of Spring, and quite as natural. I see no difficulty at all in believing that such was the charm of his personality that his mere presence could bring peace to souls in anguish, and that those who touched his garments or his hands forgot their pain: or that as he passed by on the highway of life people who had seen nothing of life's mysteries saw them clearly, and others who had been deaf to every voice but that of Pleasure heard for the first time the voice of Love and found it as "musical as is Apollo's lute"; or that evil passions fled at his approach, and men whose dull unimaginative lives had been but a mode of death rose as it were from the grave when he called them: or that when he taught on the hillside the multitude forgot their hunger and thirst and the cares of this world, and that to his friends who listened to him as he sat at meat the coarse food seemed delicate, and the water had the taste of good wine, and the whole house became full of the odour and sweetness of nard.'

And towards the end of his letter he sums up and thinks of what, if anything, the future has in store for him:

'All trials are trials for one's life, just as all sentences are sentences of death, and three times have I been tried. The first time I left the box to be arrested, the second time to be led back to the House of Detention, the third time to pass into a prison for two years. Society, as we have constituted it, will have no place for me, has none to offer; but Nature, whose sweet rains fall on unjust and just alike, will have clefts in the rocks where I may hide, and secret valleys in whose silence I may weep undisturbed. She will hang the night with stars so that I may walk abroad in the darkness without stumbling, and send the wind over my footprints so that none may track me to my hurt: she will cleanse me in great waters, and with bitter herbs make me whole.'

Wilde's release   Wilde was secretly transferred from Reading Gaol to Pentonville Prison on the evening of 18th May 1897 in order to avoid any possible demonstration by Queensberry's friends, and from there released on the morning of 19th May 1897. He was met at the gates by his faithful friend Robert Ross. According to British Prison Regulations, nothing written by a prisoner while serving his sentence is allowed to leave the gaol, except periodic letters, which are carefully scrutinised and censored by the prison authorities. However, the Governor of Reading Gaol, Major J. O. Nelson, who had done his best to make Wilde's

Lady Wilde who died whilst Oscar was in prison

Robert Ross as a young man, painted by Sir William Rothenstein

The Hôtel de la Plage (proprietor M. Bonnet), where Wilde stayed when he first came to Berneval

life more bearable during the last half of his imprisonment, disregarded the rule and gave him back his manuscript. Oscar had written to Robert Ross some time before, telling him about the letter and giving him instructions as to its disposal, and he now handed it to Ross. Thus, it will be seen that he never had an opportunity of revising or even of re-reading his manuscript. It is therefore remarkably free from inaccuracies or repetitions, particularly as it is full of quotations in various languages, none of which he had the means of verifying when he wrote them down.

Oscar Wilde travelled over to France that same evening and never set foot *Dieppe* in England again. He first stayed at Dieppe, under the assumed name of Sebastian Melmoth, which he took from a book written by his grand-uncle C. R. Maturin, the title of which was *Melmoth the Wanderer*. He was accompanied by his two great friends Robert Ross and Reginald Turner. In spite of all the hardships and humiliations from which he had suffered during his imprisonment and which had so severely affected his health that they may be said to have eventually been responsible for his death, his naturally gay nature

The house at Berneval where Wilde wrote most of *The Ballad of Reading Gaol*

soon asserted itself. Very soon after his arrival at Dieppe, he wrote to his friend Ada Leverson, who had sheltered him between his trials: 'I am staying here as Sebastian Melmoth —not Esquire but Monsieur Sébastien Melmoth. I have thought it better that Robbie should stay here under the name of Reginald Turner: and Reggie under the name of R. B. Ross. It is better that they should not have their own names.'

In Dieppe, Oscar passed a happy fortnight during which he wrote a long and moving letter to the *Daily Chronicle* on the cruelties of Prison Life; this made such a strong impression that it resulted directly in the Prisons Act of 1898, which brought about sweeping reforms in the British Prison System. With this letter his creative urge seemed to return. Ross and Turner returned to England and other friends came out to France to see him, but they all had their own business to attend to and could not stay long. He began to fret and to find the atmosphere of Dieppe unconducive to work, so he moved to the little

Berneval   village of Berneval, on the coast a few miles east of Dieppe. Here he stayed at first at the Hôtel de la Plage, but later took a small house, in which he wrote

Snapshots taken of Oscar Wilde in Rome in 1898

Oscar Wilde and
Lord Alfred Douglas
lunching in the
open air on the
Continent in 1898

most of his last serious work *The Ballad of Reading Gaol*. Thus he had begun his literary life as a poet and ended it as a poet also.

In Berneval he made himself immensely popular with everyone, including the parish priest, and on the occasion of Queen Victoria's Diamond Jubilee *Children's party* he gave a party to the local children. This is how he described the proceedings in a letter to a friend:

'My fête was a huge success: fifteen *gamins* were entertained on strawberries and cream, apricots, chocolates, cakes, and *sirop de grenadine*. I had a huge iced cake with *Jubilé de la Reine Victoria* in pink sugar just rosetted with green, and a great wreath of roses round it all. Every child was asked beforehand to choose his present: they all chose instruments of music!!!

6 *accordions,* *5 trompettes,* *4 clairons.*

They sang the Marseillaise and other songs, and danced a *ronde*, and also played "God Save the Queen": they said it was "God Save the Queen", and I did not like to differ from them. They were most gay and sweet. I gave the health of *La Reine d'Angleterre,* and they cried "*Vive la Reine d'Angleterre*". Then

The Hôtel d'Alsace, where Oscar Wilde died

Oscar Wilde's apartments in the Hôtel d'Alsace, Paris

I gave *"La France, mère de tous les artistes"*, and finally I gave *Le Président de la République*. I thought I had better do so. They cried out with one accord *"Vivent le Président de la République et Monsieur Melmoth!!!"* So I found my name coupled with that of the President. It was an amusing experience as I am hardly more than a month out of gaol.

'They stayed from 4.30 to seven o'clock and played games: on leaving I gave them each a basket with a jubilee cake frosted pink and inscribed, and *bonbons*.

'They seem to have made a great demonstration in Berneval-le-Grand, and to have gone to the house of the Mayor and cried *"Vive Monsieur le Maire! Vive le Reine d'Angleterre! Vive Monsieur Melmoth!"* I tremble at my position.'

However, the intervals between visits from his friends became longer and longer, and Wilde began to feel desperately lonely. Then Alfred Douglas, to whom he had addressed *De Profundis*, who had been responsible for his downfall and whom he had declared his intention of never seeing again, came to visit him, and they went off to Italy together; there he finished *The Ballad of*

'The Ballad of Reading Gaol'

Sir Travers Humphreys, who took part as a junior counsel in the 1895 trials and in later life declared that the prosecution of Oscar Wilde ought never to have been brought

Reading Gaol, and there he gradually realised that he could never write again under his own name.

Lady Wilde, his mother, had died at the beginning of 1896, while he was in prison; the news was broken to him by his wife, who travelled specially to Reading from Italy to do so. In April 1898 his wife died too, and he himself did not long survive her. In May 1899 he returned finally to Paris, where he took rooms at the Hôtel d'Alsace. By this time he had realised that the future held nothing for him, particularly in his own lifetime, and he made no effort to do any more creative work. In the middle of the following year he began to suffer from intermittent headaches of a progressively severe nature, and on 30th November 1900 he died in the Hôtel d'Alsace, fortified by the rites of the Catholic Church, into which he had been received on the previous day. On his death certificate the cause of death was given as 'cerebral meningitis'. He was buried three days later at Bagneux Cemetery, in the presence of Robert Ross, Reginald Turner, and Alfred Douglas. In 1909 his remains were removed to the French

Death of Lady Wilde

Death of Oscar Wilde

National Cemetery of Père Lachaise, where they now repose beneath the famous Epstein monument. And in 1954, to commemorate the hundredth anniversary of Oscar Wilde's birth, the London County Council placed a plaque on the house in Tite Street where he lived and worked between 1884 and 1895.

The tragedy of Oscar Wilde ranks with most other great historical tragedies, which are mainly brought about by the stupidity of pompous and self-important people—in this case Mr Justice Wills, in whose power it was to bind Oscar Wilde over instead of submitting his sensitive soul to two years' unnecessary torture. Nearly sixty years later, in 1954, Sir Travers Humphreys, one of the kindest and wisest judges who has ever sat on the English Bench and who had himself, as a very junior barrister, taken part in the trials, wrote in his reminiscences; 'Reflecting upon the events of nearly sixty years ago, one fact is plain beyond argument. The prosecution of Oscar Wilde should never have been brought.'

In the first two years of his marriage, Oscar Wilde's wife Constance bore him two sons. They never saw their father again after the events of 1895. The elder, Cyril, adopted the army as his career and was killed by a German sniper's bullet in France in 1915. The younger, Vyvyan, is the writer of the present chronicle.

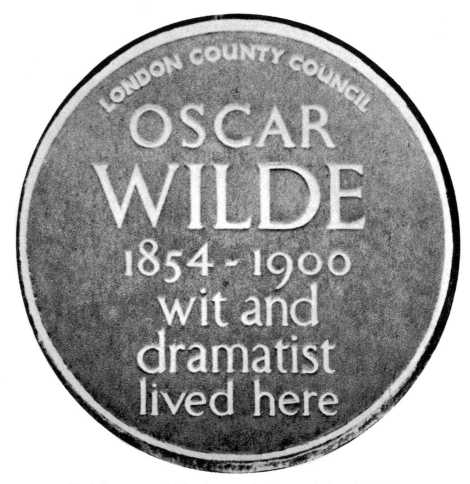

The final gesture, on 16th October 1954, the plaque on the house in Tite Street

1854 Oscar Fingal O'Flahertie Wills Wilde was born on 16th October at No. 21 Westland Row, Dublin. He was the second son of Sir William Wilde, a prominent oculist and aural surgeon, and his wife Jane Francesca Elgee, an ardent Irish patriot who, before her marriage, wrote inflammatory political articles under the pseudonym 'Speranza'.

1864 At Portora Royal School, Enniskillen, Wilde was not very popular among the boys. Although chided repeatedly by his masters for idleness he won, in his last year at school, the Portora Gold Medal for the best classical scholar.

1871 When just seventeen Oscar gained an entrance scholarship to Trinity College, Dublin. It was here that he met John Pentland Mahaffy, Junior Fellow, Junior Dean, and Professor of Ancient History.

1874 The Berkeley Gold Medal for Greek, the highest classical award obtainable at Trinity College, Dublin, was presented to Oscar Wilde. In the same year he won a scholarship to Magdalen College, Oxford. John Ruskin, Slade Professor of Art, Walter Pater, and Cardinal Newman were to exert much influence on this twenty-year-old undergraduate.

1875 Whilst touring in Italy during the summer vacation Wilde wrote one of his earliest known poems, *San Miniato*. It was not published until several years later.

1876 Sir William Wilde died and Lady Wilde moved to England.

1877 Wilde, in company with two other young men, was taken on a tour of Greece by Professor Mahaffy.

1878 The last year at Oxford ended triumphantly, for not only did Oscar go down with a 'Double First' but he won the Newdigate Prize with his poem on Ravenna. The prize poem is printed in book form at the expense of the University and *Ravenna* became the first published work of Wilde. From Oxford Oscar moved to London where he set himself up as Professor of Aesthetics.

1880 By now Oscar was becoming conspicuous in London society and *Punch* soon began to make mock of his appearance. His first play *Vera* was written in this year but was not staged in London.

1881 The operatic skit on Aestheticism, *Patience*, by W. S. Gilbert and Arthur Sullivan brought Wilde an unintended notoriety. In this year appeared a collection of his poems, possibly published at his own expense.

1882 Wilde was invited to make a lecture tour in America. He landed at New York on 2nd January and spent twelve months travelling the length and breadth of the country addressing meetings of society ladies, students, and even miners. His audiences were delighted by his charm, his wit, his voice, and his elegance, but the critics were hostile.

1883 February and March found Oscar Wilde in Paris completing *The Duchess of Padua*. This play had been written at the request of the actress Mary Anderson but she did not like the finished work—a severe blow for the author, who was in some financial need. On 20th August Wilde was present at the first performance of *Vera* at the Union Square Theatre, New York. The play was a failure and was withdrawn within a week.

1884 Wilde's marriage to Constance Mary Lloyd, daughter of a well-known Irish Q.C., took place on 29th May. The honeymoon was spent in Paris and the couple then moved into No. 16 Tite Street.

1885 Now Wilde had not only himself and his wife to support, but a son, Cyril. It was thus imperative that he should find employment. He became book reviewer on the *Pall Mall Gazette* and frequently contributed to other magazines and reviews.

1886 Wilde's second son, Vyvyan, was born this year. From 1886, too, dates Wilde's friendship with Robert Ross, a friendship that was to survive disgrace and imprisonment, and remain lifelong.

1887 For the next two years Wilde was editor of *The Woman's World*. He also wrote and had published some short stories.

1888 An excellent raconteur to children as well as grown-ups—in this year appeared a collection of fairy-tales under the title *The Happy Prince and Other Tales.*

1891 Four books of very differing character were published this year—*A House of Pomegranates, Lord Arthur Savile's Crime, Intentions,* and *The Picture of Dorian Gray.* The latter caused a great furore and was very adversely received by the Press. The acquaintance with Lord Alfred Douglas, which was to have such a disastrous outcome, began.

1892 The first performance of *Lady Windermere's Fan* took place on 20th February with George Alexander, Lily Hanbury, and Marion Terry playing the leading parts. *Salomé,* written in French and then translated into English, was put into rehearsal by Sarah Bernhardt but the Lord Chamberlain refused a licence on the grounds that no

Biblical character should appear on the stage.

1893 On 19th April the Haymarket Theatre opened with *A Woman of No Importance* starring Sir Herbert Beerbohm Tree and Mrs Bernard Beere. The play met with immediate success. However, Wilde was still more acclaimed in France, whither he went later that year, than at home. In June John Lane and the Bodley Head publishing house brought out, in a beautiful production, *The Sphinx.*

1895 The Prince of Wales was present at the opening night of *An Ideal Husband,* on 3rd January. It was rare for royalty to attend such an event and the Prince was delighted with the performance, declaring that not one single word should be altered. 14th February saw the curtains open on Wilde's last and greatest comedy, *The Importance of Being Earnest.* Wilde had reached the zenith of his career—disaster was to follow. On 18th February the Marquess of Queensberry left the fatal card bearing the words 'To Oscar Wilde, posing as a somdomite' at the Albemarle Club. Ten days later it was found by Wilde who applied for a warrant for the arrest of the Marquess.

Wilde returned from visiting Monte Carlo with Lord Alfred Douglas for the opening of the Marquess's trial on 3rd April before Mr Justice Henn Collins. After three days a verdict of 'Not Guilty' was returned. That same day Wilde was arrested and charged at Bow Street under a section of the Criminal Law Amendment Act of 1885. He was held at Holloway Gaol until the trial opened on 26th April. Meanwhile an 'auction' at his home, No. 16 Tite Street, had been an excuse for pillage and devastation. Mr Justice Charles presided at this first trial of Wilde on which a verdict of 'Not Guilty' was passed on certain counts. He was re-charged and on 20th May a second trial opened before Mr Justice Wills. It resulted in a verdict of 'Guilty' and Wilde was sentenced to two years' imprisonment with hard labour. This sentence was served first at Wandsworth and then in Reading Gaol.

1896–97 During his imprisonment Wilde wrote an explanation of his conduct in the form of a letter to Lord Alfred Douglas, *De Profundis*. The prison authorities would only allow him one sheet of paper at a time and Wilde was never able to re-read or revise this work which contains some of the most beautiful of his prose. In 1896 Constance Wilde visited Oscar to break the news of the death of Lady Wilde. This was to be the last meeting of husband and wife. One slight joy illuminated these grim years. News came that *Salomé* had been staged in Paris by Lugne-Poë.

1897 On his release from prison Robert Ross accompanied Wilde to France. For a while he settled in Berneval under the name of Sebastian Melmoth. He wrote his best-known poem, *The Ballad of Reading Gaol*.

1898 The death of Constance Wilde. Oscar wandered around France, Italy, and Switzerland, sometimes with Lord Alfred Douglas, sometimes accompanied by Ross or another friend, often alone.

1900 On 30th November, the day after he was received into the Roman Catholic Church, Oscar Wilde died. He was buried at Bagneux Cemetery in the presence of Robert Ross, Reginald Turner, and Alfred Douglas.

1909 His remains were removed to the French National Cemetery of Père Lachaise, where his body now rests.

BIBLIOGRAPHY

Wilde's collected works were edited and published by his friend Robert Ross in 1908. A useful one-volume edition of the complete works with an introduction by Vyvyan Holland was published in 1966. Plays, poems and prose are all widely available in paperback in various editions.

CRITICAL WRITINGS AND LETTERS

Rupert Hart-Davis has edited Wilde's letters in two volumes, *The Letters of Oscar Wilde* (1962) and *More Letters of Oscar Wilde* (1985). A *Selected Letters*, including the complete text of *De Profundis*, is available in paperback, also edited by Hart-Davis (1979). Wilde's own critical writings are collected and edited by Richard Ellmann in *The Artist as Critic* (1982), and criticism of Wilde is surveyed in an annotated bibliography by E. K. Mikhail (1914; reprinted 1967). Wilde's holograph text of *The Importance of being Earnest* was published in facsimile in 1950. The standard bibliography of Wilde's works is by Stuart Mason (1914; reprinted 1967).

LIFE AND TIMES

Richard Ellmann's excellent *Oscar Wilde* (1987) is the standard biography, but it does not entirely supplant Hesketh Pearson's *Life of Oscar Wilde* (1946). Frank Harris's *Oscar Wilde: His Life and Confessions* (1930) is generally held to be unreliable and unpleasantly self-centred, but it does include some of Wilde's letters and contributions from Robert Ross, Bernard Shaw and Lord Alfred Douglas.

Wilde's uneasy relationship with his audience is the subject of *Idylls of the Marketplace: Oscar Wilde and the Victorian Public* by Regenia Gagnier (1987). Wilde's travels are chronicled by Lloyd Lewis and Henry Justin Smith in *Oscar Wilde Discovers America* (1936), to which can be added *Oscar Wilde in Canada* (1982) by Kevin O'Brien. *Impressions of America by Oscar Wilde*, edited by Stuart Mason (1906) sets down Wilde's own pensées, and conversations with Wilde are recorded by Laurence Housman in *Écho de Paris* (1923). Stuart Mason also gives us *Oscar Wilde, Three Times Tried* and *Art and Morality* (both 1912). Transcripts of the trials are edited by H. Montgomery Hyde in *The Trials of Oscar Wilde* (1948). The repercussions of the trials, the break-up of Wilde's estate, etc. are described by him in *Oscar Wilde, The Aftermath* (1963). Rupert Croft Cooke's *The Unrecorded Life of Oscar Wilde* (1972) contains much material unpublished anywhere else.

PEOPLE

A good modern account of Sir William and Lady Wilde is Eric Lambert's *Mad with Much Heart, a life of the Parents of Oscar Wilde* (1967). *Speranza, a biography of Lady Wilde* by Horace Wyndham was published in 1951. Wilde's relationship with his mother is explored by Anna de Brémont in *Oscar Wilde and His Mother* (1911).

Constance Wilde is the subject of a modern biography by Anne Clark Amor, *Mrs Oscar Wilde: A Woman of Some Importance* (1983), and Vyvyan Holland describes his relationship with his father in *Son of Oscar Wilde* (1954).

Bosie spent the majority of his life picking over and publishing defences of his relationship with Wilde. His *Autobiography* appeared in 1929 and three other titles are *Oscar Wilde and Myself* (1914), *Without Apology* (1938) and *Oscar Wilde: A Summing Up* (1962). A full modern account is *Bosie* by Rupert Croft Cooke (1963).

Margery Ross edited a collection of letters to her uncle in *Robert Ross, Friend of Friends* (1952). Ada Leverson published *Letters to the Sphinx from Oscar Wilde, with Reminiscences of the Author* in 1930. Max Beerbohm's *Letters to Reggie Turner* are edited by Rupert Hart-Davis (1964). The latter is also the subject of a biography, *Reggie, A Portrait of Reginald Turner* by Stanley Weintraub (1965). Rupert Hart-Davis has also published a selection of Max Beerbohm's letters (1988).

ILLUSTRATED EDITIONS.

Wilde's works, especially *Salomé*, continue to seduce artists and illustrators. A 1938 edition of the play features drawings by the Fauvist painter André Derain, and Aubrey Beardsley's controversial decorations for the 1894 edition have been reproduced many times. *The Picture of Dorian Gray* was published in 1908 in an edition with etchings from drawings by Paul Thiriat.

NOTES ON THE PICTURES

Frontispiece. OSCAR WILDE photographed in c. 1891 by W. & D. Downy.

Page

5 A PICTURESQUE AND DESCRIPTIVE VIEW OF THE CITY OF DUBLIN; a view of the city from Magazine Hill in Phoenix Park. An eighteenth-century print. *By courtesy of the Trustees of the British Museum, London.*

6 WILDE'S FATHER at the age of twenty-eight. A portrait by Bernard Mulrenin (1803–1868), the well-known Irish portrait painter, Member of the Royal Hibernian Academy. *Present location unknown.*

7 SIR WILLIAM WILDE AND SIR WILLIAM STOKES. Sir William Stokes was the son of William Stokes who had taught Wilde at the Dublin School of Medicine. He was an eminent physician, and physician to Queen Victoria in Ireland. A contemporary photograph. *Collection the author.*

8 SIR WILLIAM WILDE. From H. Wyndham, *Victorian Sensations*, London, 1933. *By permission of Jarrolds Ltd.*

9 WILDE'S MOTHER, painted by Bernard Mulrenin. *Present location unknown.*

10 OSCAR WILDE, aged about two. In those days boys were usually kept in skirts until they were three or even older. A coloured Daguerreotype. *Collection the author.*

11 21, WESTLAND ROW, DUBLIN. *By courtesy of the Irish Tourist Board.*

13 1, MERRION SQUARE, DUBLIN. From the drawing-room window Wilde could look out over an extensive square, three sides of which were formed of houses such as this.

On the west side was Leinster House. *By courtesy of the Irish Tourist Board.*

ENVELOPE CONTAINING A LOCK OF ISOLA FRANCESCA WILDE'S HAIR. Her death at the age of ten in 1867 caused much grief not only to Lady Wilde who had always wanted a daughter, but also to Oscar. *Collection the author.*

14 LOUGH CORRIB, COUNTY MAYO. Here as a schoolboy and a young man Wilde fished, rode, and learned to love the country. Behind Moytura House are the Moycullen Hills; the sunshine produces colours of surpassing beauty. *By courtesy of the Irish Tourist Board.*

15 CONG RIVER AND ASHFORD, a drawing by Wakeman engraved by Oldham from Sir William Wilde's *Lough Corrib*, McGlashan and Gill of Dublin and Longmans Green and Co. London, 1867.

16 TRINITY COLLEGE, DUBLIN. The earliest surviving portion dates from 1722. The architects of the Palladian façade (1759) were two Londoners, Henry Keene (1726–1776) and John Sanderson. Aquatint by James Malton, dated 1797. *By courtesy of the Trustees of the British Museum, London.*

17 THE REV. SIR JOHN PENTLAND MAHAFFY (1839–1919), Professor of Ancient History at Trinity College, Dublin, became Provost of his College in 1914. From 1911 to 1916 he was President of the Royal Irish Academy and in 1918 he was awarded the C.B.E. for his defence of Trinity College during the Irish Rebellion of 1916. A contemporary photograph. *Private collection.*

THE BERKELEY GOLD MEDAL for Greek is awarded annually for the best thesis on a set subject. *By courtesy of the National Museum of Ireland.*

18 MAGDALEN COLLEGE, OXFORD, was founded in 1474 by William Waynefleet, Bishop of Winchester. An early nineteenth-century engraving of the College seen from across the Cherwell. *By permission of the National Building Record.*

19 JOHN HENRY NEWMAN (1801–1890) was leader of the Oxford Movement which aimed at deepening spiritual life within the Church of England. He joined the Roman Catholic Church in 1845 and was made a Cardinal in 1879. This drawing in chalk by George Richmond (1809–1896) was made about 1840. *By courtesy of the Trustees of the National Portrait Gallery, London.*

JOHN RUSKIN (1819–1900), the eminent English writer and critic who influenced English art criticism for a whole generation. Carlyle called his *Stones of Venice* 'a singular sign of the times', 'a new Renaissance'. Oscar Wilde had come under his spell and was amongst those Oxford undergraduates who helped Ruskin on his road-building adventure. A drawing in chalk by George Richmond. *By courtesy of the Trustees of the National Portrait Gallery, London.*

20 WALTER PATER (1839–1894) was elected to a fellowship at Brasenose College, Oxford, in 1864. His study of *Aesthetic Poetry* appeared in 1868 and he became the centre of a small circle in Oxford which included the group of Pre-Raphaelites. He is chiefly remembered for his aesthetic approach to life. *Photo: Elliot and Fry, London.*

21 FRIENDS OF WILDE AT OXFORD, from left to right: E. C. Jones, E. L. Jeffrey, C. H. Allenby, and W. W. Ward. A contemporary photograph. *Private collection.*

AT OXFORD Oscar Wilde lived the normal life of an undergraduate, playing games, drinking a little, cutting lectures, and flirting. A contemporary photograph. *Private collection.*

A CONTEMPORARY PHOTOGRAPH taken in the grounds of Magdalen College, Oxford. *From the Dorothy Sayers family album.*

22 A MING VASE in 'blue and white' porcelain from the collection of George Thompson. This illustration was by Whistler for the catalogue of Thompson's Collection, one of the first collections of Ming in Great Britain. The butterfly on the right is Whistler's mark. When at Oxford Wilde took up the fashion and decorated his rooms at Magdalen with 'blue and white'. From M. Marks, *Catalogue of Blue and White Porcelain after Whistler, 1878.*

WILDE'S ROOMS AT MAGDALEN. A contemporary photograph. *From W. W. Ward's family album.*

23 WILDE'S COLLEGE FRIENDS: J. Peyton, C. A. Swan, C. H. Tindal, and R. S. B. Hammond Chambers. *Private collection.*

24 DANTE'S TOMB AT RAVENNA which Wilde visited on his tour of Italy. An engraving by E. Finder from a drawing by S. Prout. *By courtesy of the Mansell Collection.*

25 THE FORUM, ROME. A contemporary photograph. *Private collection.*

26 OSCAR WILDE photographed in Greek costume in Athens, which he visited in 1877 with Professor Mahaffy. *Collection the author.*

WILDE IN VENETIAN COSTUME. A contemporary photograph. *Collection the author.*

27 OSCAR WILDE photographed during his Oxford days. *Radio Times Hulton Picture Library.*

RAVENNA. The cover. The Newdigate Prize Poem was printed at the University's expense by Thomas Shrimpton and Son, Broad Street, Oxford, 1878. Photograph of a presentation copy by the author.

28 LILY LANGTRY (1852–1929) was for many years considered the most beautiful woman in England and known as 'the Jersey Lily'. She appeared on the stage in both England and America under her own management from 1881. Sir Max Beerbohm cited her amongst his four examples of the 'professional beauty'. *Photo: W. and D. Downey, London. Thames and Hudson Archives.*

29 VERA was given a first performance at the Union Square Theatre in New York on 20th August 1883, but it was not a success.

30, 31 THE AESTHETIC MOVEMENT lampooned by *Punch. Punch* had been founded in 1841 as a satirical weekly. The three cartoons reproduced here are all by George du Maurier (1834–1896), a Frenchman by birth, who settled in London and made himself a name as a caricaturist. Already by 1877 du Maurier had begun to satirise the cult of Aestheticism and two years later began his series entitled 'Nincompoopiana'. In the cartoon of 14th February 1880, a long-haired, poetic-faced Mr Postlethwaite (maybe Wilde, maybe Swinburne) is being fawned over by ladies and gentlemen alike. 'Algernon' on the 'Six-Mark Teapot' has a likeness to Swinburne, although the idea of 'living up to one's blue china' is Wilde's. The third cartoon appeared in *Punch,* 9th October 1880.

33 PATIENCE a comic operetta which satirised the Aesthetic Movement, with words by W. S. Gilbert and music by Arthur Sullivan. It was first produced in 1881. *Radio Times Hulton Picture Library.*

34 THE COVER OF A SONG by Robert Coote, published by Hopwood and Crew, London. The wrapper of the *Patience Lancers,* a dance-tune by Charles d'Albert. *By courtesy of Chappell and Co. Ltd, London.*

35 YE SOUL AGONIES. The cover of a satire sold for ten cents on the American railways. On the reverse is written: 'Published by P.O. Box 2678. Address Publisher. Entered according to Act of Congress in the year 1882, in he office of the Librarian of Congress, at Washington.'

36 JAY'S OPERA HOUSE, KANSAS, where Wilde lectured on 'Art Decoration' to a meagre audience on 18th April 1882.

37 WASHINGTON IRVING lived at one time in this house at the corner of Irving Place and 17th Street, New York; Wilde stayed in the house adjoining on the left. From Martin Birnbaum, *Oscar Wilde Fragments and Memories,* Elkin Matthews, London, 1920.

38 OSCAR WILDE sketched at his opening lecture and at a New York reception; drawings by a staff artist for *Frank Leslie's Illustrated Newspaper,* 21st January 1882.

PATIENCE; Gilbert and Sullivan's operettas had as great a success in America as in Britain and performances were staged by numerous pirate companies. Even the comic figures on this advertisement in *The Cincinnati Enquirer* were copied from D'Oyly Carte's programme.

39 GEORGE MAXWELL ROBESON sketched in the House of Representatives by John W. Alexander. Robeson was host to Oscar Wilde in Washington. The sketch appeared in *Harper's Weekly,* 8th April 1882.

40 WILDE VISITED Mobile, Alabama, on 28th June 1882. A contemporary photograph. *Collection the author.*

41 PARIS, the Porte St Martin and the Boulevard St Denis in the 1880s. *Photo: Collection Yvan Christ, Paris.*

42 ROBERT HARBOROUGH SHERARD, Wilde's earliest biographer, from whose writings nearly all subsequent biographies have sprung. *Photo : Harris Picture Agency, London.*

43 MARY ANDERSON (1859–1940), American actress, made her début on the stage as Juliet in Louisville at the age of sixteen. From 1883 to 1889, when she retired from the stage, Mary Anderson played for several seasons in London. At the opening of the Shakespeare Memorial Theatre at Stratford-on-Avon (1877) she played the part of Rosalind in *As You Like It*. Engraving, 1883. *Thames and Hudson Archives.*

44 PAUL VERLAINE (1844–1896) was one of the Parnassian poets, but his symbolist pagan beginnings are less well remembered than the passionate yet religious poems of *Sagesse* (1881). His life was tragic; his friendship with Rimbaud was ill-starred and broke up his family life. He spent his last years in drunkenness and poverty in Paris. A contemporary photograph. *Radio Times Hulton Picture Library.*

VICTOR HUGO (1802–1885) was the greatest Romantic literary figure in nineteenth-century France. His play *Hernani* (1830) had a *succès de scandale* and marked the beginning of a new era in French drama; his sonorous prose and poetry, subjective and sensuous, was part of a Romantic attitude which eventually led to the trend towards Aestheticism at the end of the century. Contemporary photograph. *Radio Times Hulton Picture Library.*

45 EMILE ZOLA (1840–1902) became, on the publication of *L'Assommoir*, the most discussed novelist in France. Other successes followed including *Nana* (1880) and *La Débâcle* (1892). Zola espoused the cause of Dreyfus, impeached the military authorities and was sentenced in 1898 to imprisonment, but escaped for a year to England. He was later able to return to Paris where he passed the last three years of his life. The Impressionist painter Edouard Manet (1832–1883) painted this portrait which now hangs in the Jeu de Paume, Paris. *Photo : Giraudon.*

46 MINERS AT FOOT OF SHAFT, Leadville, Colorado. Here, by custom, each man carried a revolver. When warned that his own life and that of his travelling manager might be in danger, Wilde replied that nothing they could do to his manager would intimidate him. This illustration appeared in *The Daily Graphic*, New York, on 22nd March 1882.

47 THE LEADVILLE MINERS were described by Wilde as 'The only well-dressed men I have seen in America.' The cartoon 'Something to "Live Up" to in America', by Thomas Nast, appeared in *Harper's Bazaar,* 10th June 1882.

48 THE MORMON TABERNACLE which Wilde visited during his stay in Salt Lake City in April 1882. From H. G. Marshall *Through America*, London, 1882.

THE BALLOON CAR, American public transport. From H. G. Marshall, *Through America*, London, 1882.

49 JAMES ABBOTT MCNEILL WHISTLER (1834–1903). Whistler left his native America for Europe in 1855. After some years in France where he mixed with the Impressionist painters, he came to London and had a brilliant career as a painter and art theorist, although his sharp wit and arrogant behaviour gained him many enemies. This drawing by Leslie Ward (the cartoonist Spy) is in the National Portrait Gallery, London. *By courtesy of the National Magazine Company.*

50 OSCAR WILDE. A chalk drawing of about 1883. *Collection the author.*

51 CONSTANCE MARY LLOYD was a very beautiful and talented woman. Although she never wrote an important book, she was a frequent contributor to contemporary magazines. *Collection the author.*

52 ST JAMES'S CHURCH, PADDINGTON, was rebuilt in 1881 by Street on the foundations of an earlier church dating from 1841 to 1843. It is the earlier church, designed by Goldicutt and Gutch, which is reproduced in this engraving. The old chancel became, in Street's renovation, the west chapel. Engraving 1841. *By courtesy of Paddington Public Library.*

53 16, TITE STREET, CHELSEA, was built about 1860. Whistler and Sargent had their studios in this street and Mr Justice Wills, who was to pronounce sentence on Wilde in 1895, lived there; however, the west side of the street backed on to some of the most wretched of the Chelsea slums. From Lord Alfred Douglas, *Oscar Wilde and Myself*, John Long Ltd, London, 1914.

54 MRS PATRICK CAMPBELL (1865–1940) gained her first great success in *The Second Mrs Tanqueray* by Pinero in 1893. Other parts for which she is famous were in Davidson's *For the Crown* and as Eliza in Shaw's *Pygmalion*. She also played Magda in Sudermann's play. Charles Haslewood Shannon (1865–1937) painted this portrait in 1908. *By courtesy of the Trustees of the Tate Gallery, London.*

55 ELLEN TERRY'S (1847–1928) long partnership with Henry Irving—in the course of which she played the lead in many of Shakespeare's plays—dated from 1878. With the Lyceum Company she several times visited the United States. In 1925 she received the Grand Cross of the Order of the British Empire. This photograph was taken by Julia Margaret Cameron. *By courtesy of the Metropolitan Museum of Art, Alfred Stieglitz Collection, through Miss Georgia O'Keeffe, 1949.*

56 SOCIETY was sub-titled 'A Weekly Journal of General Literature for the Upper and Middle Classes'. The journal was inaugurated on the 24th January 1878 and appeared until 1900 when the magazine was discontinued. The editor, Arthur Goddard, only obtained one contribution from Wilde, 'Roses and Rue'.

57 OSCAR WILDE is the tall figure to the right of *The Private View of the Academy* by William Powell Frith (1819–1909), which is now in the collection of A. C. R. Pope, Esq., Dorchester. Although Frith was to die in poverty and loneliness he was for a time the most popular painter of his day. He became an Associate of the Royal Academy in 1845 and a Member eight years later. Best known of his paintings, which often depict scenes of everyday life, is *Derby Day*. *By courtesy of A. C. R. Pope, Esq., Dorchester.*

58 ROBERT BROWNING (1812–1889) gained fame as a poet rather than as a playwright. Among his writings are *The Ring and the Book* published in four volumes in 1868–1869, *Paracelsus* (1835), and *Sordello* (1840). This portrait, dated 1875, is by George Frederick Watts (1817–1904). *By courtesy of the Trustees of the National Portrait Gallery, London.*

'MARK TWAIN' was the pen-name of Samuel Longhorne Clemens (1835–1910). He was probably the most characteristic American writer of his time and, in the last ten years of his life, a most conspicuous and picturesque figure. To English readers he is best known for his *Adventures of Tom Sawyer* and *Huckleberry Finn*. His humour is given full reign in the account of his European travels, *A Tramp Abroad*. *Radio Times Hulton Picture Library.*

59 SARAH BERNHARDT (1845–1923) made her début at the Comédie-Française in 1862. Her performance as Phèdre in Racine's play of that name and as Doña Sol in Victor Hugo's *Hernani* displayed to the full the power of her emotional acting and the magnetism of her personality. The first of many visits to London was in 1879 when she had a season at the

Gaiety Theatre. This photograph was taken about 1885. *Photo: Collection Yvan Christ, Paris.*

60 A VIGNETTE from *The Woman's World*, vol. III, 1889, possibly by Charles Ricketts. For two years Wilde, as editor, persuaded well-known artists and writers to contribute. *By courtesy of the Trustees of the British Museum, London.*

61 MRS WILDE assisting at a bazaar. *Radio Times Hulton Picture Library.*

62 THE LADY'S WORLD was renamed *The Woman's World* five months after Wilde became editor. This illustration appeared in the first volume, 1887. *By courtesy of the Trustees of the British Museum, London.*

THE WOMAN'S WORLD. The title-page of vol. II, 1888. *By courtesy of the Trustees of the British Museum, London.*

63 THE POEM BY BEATRICE and design by Walter Crane in *The Woman's World*, vol. II, 1888. *By courtesy of the Trustees of the British Museum, London.*

ELLEN TERRY as Lady Macbeth. A reproduction from *The Women's World*, vol. III, 1889. *By courtesy of the Trustees of the British Museum, London.*

64 CONSTANCE WILDE and her son Cyril in 1891. *Collection the author.*

65 THERE WAS ONCE, a collection of stories by Constance Wilde published in 1889. Title-page. *By courtesy of the Trustees of the British Museum, London.*

67 OSCAR WILDE drawn by William Speed at a hearing of the Parnell Commission in 1888. *By courtesy of the Victoria and Albert Museum, London.*

68 FRANK HARRIS, journalist and fellow Irishman, whose scandal-mongering biography of Wilde, *Oscar Wilde: His Life and Confessions*, was published in 1930. *Radio Times Hulton Picture Library.*

69 THE PICTURE OF DORIAN GREY, published in 1891 remained Oscar Wilde's only novel.

71 'A PEEP INTO THE PAST', a humorous essay, was written by Max Beerbohm for the first number of the *Yellow Book* in 1894, but was replaced at the last moment by his famous essay on 'Defence of Cosmetics', possibly because of the impending Wilde scandal—Wilde's friends were already growing anxious about his reckless behaviour. 'A Peep into the Past' was eventually published in a limited private edition in 1923. *By courtesy of the Trustees of the British Museum, London, and Messrs William Heinemann, London.*

72 EDWARD HENRY CARSON (1854–1935) became a Q.C. at the Irish Bar in 1889. Called to the English bar, he was even more successful than in his own country. Although he had been returned to Parliament in 1882 it was only when the Home Rule Bill—of which he was a strong opponent—was proposed in 1911 that he began to play a prominent part in politics. In 1915 he held the post of Attorney-General and, the following year, became First Lord of the Admiralty. In 1921 he was raised to the peerage. This etching by John George Day was made in 1913. *By courtesy of the Trustees of the National Portrait Gallery, London.*

73 OSCAR WILDE at the height of his fame, a contemporary photograph. *Collection the author.*

75 JOHN SINGER SARGENT was a visitor to 16 Tite Street. *By courtesy of the Trustees of the Tate Gallery, London, and the Executors of the Estate of the late Sir Max Beerbohm.*

76 A HOUSE OF POMEGRANATES. The title-page. Charles Ricketts (1866–1931), best

known for his stage designs and an Associate of the Royal Academy for the last nine years of his life, carried out the decorative design. The illustrations are by Charles Haslewood Shannon (1865–1937) who became a Member of the Royal Academy in 1911. The book was published by James R. Osgood, McIlvaine and Company of London in 1891.

77 ALGERNON CHARLES SWINBURNE (1837–1909). Contemporary of Whistler's, friend of Rossetti, Swinburne saw much of the Pre-Raphaelites, sharing their enthusiasms and expressing their ideals in his verse. He was a frequent visitor at Tite Street. G. F. Watts painted this portrait in 1886. *By courtesy of the Trustees of the National Portrait Gallery, London.*

78 WALT WHITMAN (1819–1892). Wilde met Whitman in Philadelphia in 1882. Whitman found the Englishman 'genuine, honest, and manly'. Wilde, who had admired the American's verse since childhood and had looked forward eagerly to this meeting, said 'I have come to you as one with whom I have been acquainted almost from the cradle', he was later to call Whitman 'the simplest and strongest man I ever met'. *Radio Times Hulton Picture Library.*

WALTER CRANE (1845–1915), the English artist, was much influenced by the Pre-Raphaelites and by Ruskin, whose student he was.

79 THE PROGRAMME for *Lady Windermere's Fan,* first produced at the St James's Theatre in 1892. *Thames and Hudson Archives.*

80 LADY WINDERMERE'S FAN. A scene from the play. *The Enthoven Collection. By courtesy of the Victoria and Albert Museum, London.*

81 GEORGE ALEXANDER with Lily Hanbury in a later production of *Lady Windermere's Fan. The Enthoven Collection. By courtesy of the Victoria and Albert Museum, London.*

NUTCOMBE GOULD and Marion Terry in *Lady Windermere's Fan. The Enthoven Collection. By courtesy of the Victoria and Albert Museum, London.*

83 ST JAMES'S THEATRE was demolished in 1958 to make way for an office block. *By courtesy of the National Buildings Record.*

84 WILDE'S SALOMÉ was more influenced by the theme as depicted in paintings than by the actual Bible story. *Salomé* was not produced in England until 1905 although it was much acclaimed in France, Germany, and other non-English-speaking countries. Wallpainting, Bellinge Church on Funen. *By courtesy of the Danish National Museum, Copenhagen.*

85 'THE PEACOCK SKIRT', one of the book illustrations by Aubrey Vincent Beardsley (1872–1898), for the first edition of *Salomé* published in 1894 by Elkin Matthews and John Lane. Beardsley's originality places him among the most interesting figures in the history of book illustration. At one time attracted to the Pre-Raphaelites, he later was influenced by the art of Japan, ancient Greece, and eighteenth-century France. *By permission of The Bodley Head, London.*

86 SALOMÉ was considered by Ross 'the most powerful and perfect of all Oscar's dramas'. The half title drawn by Aubrey Beardsley.

87 OSCAR WILDE and the Lord Chamberlain, a cartoon by Harry Furniss for *Cassell's Christmas Annual, 1892.*

88 BERNARD PARTRIDGE'S (1861–1945) CARICATURE of Wilde in the uniform of a private in the French army. When the licence for *Salomé* was refused Wilde had threatened to become a French citizen. Partridge joined the staff of *Punch* in 1891 and became its chief cartoonist. He was knighted in 1925. *Collection the author.*

HERBERT BEERBOHM TREE (1853–1917) was a half-brother of Max Beerbohm, the writer and caricaturist. His first professional performance was in 1876. In 1887 he became manager of the Haymarket Theatre, London, and, ten years later, of Her Majesty's Theatre. In 1907 he established a school of drama in London. He was knighted in 1909. This drawing is by Harry Furniss. *By courtesy of the Trustees of the National Portrait Gallery, London.*

89 THE PROGRAMME for the first performance of *A Woman of No Importance* at the Haymarket Theatre. *Thames and Hudson Archives.*

90 A WOMAN OF NO IMPORTANCE, a scene from the play drawn by Raymond Potter for *The Illustrated London News* at a production at the Haymarket Theatre on 19th April 1893. *By Courtesy of The Illustrated London News and the Victoria and Albert Museum, London.*

91 WILDE at a dinner to some Montmartre poets. *Collection the author.*

A POSTER by Henri de Toulouse-Lautrec (1864–1901), the French lithographer, advertising the Moulin Rouge where La Goulue was to perform. *Crown Copyright. By courtesy of the Victoria and Albert Museum, London.*

92 LORD ALFRED DOUGLAS inscribed this photograph to Oscar Wilde. *Present location unknown.*

93 THE SPHINX was written over the course of eight years. Published in June 1893, it was elaborately produced, on hand-made paper and in different coloured inks. The designs were by Charles Ricketts. The title-page. Wilde: *The Sphinx*, Elkin Matthews and John Lane, London, 1894.

94 AUTOGRAPH from *The Sphinx*, from Stuart Mason, *Bibliography of Oscar Wilde*, London, 1914.

95 PROGRAMME of the original production of *An Ideal Husband*. *Thames and Hudson Archives.*

96 LEWIS WALLER and Julia Neilson in a production of *An Ideal Husband* on 3rd January 1895. *The Enthoven Collection. By courtesy of the Victoria and Albert Museum, London.*

97 GEORGE BERNARD SHAW (1856–1950) was art, music, then drama critic between 1885 and 1898 for several papers and magazines, including the *Pall Mall Gazette* and the *Saturday Review,* in which he reviewed Wilde's plays. This photograph was taken in about 1885. *Radio Times Hulton Picture Library.*

98 PROGRAMME for the first performance of *The Importance of Being Earnest* at the St James's Theatre, of which George Alexander was the manager. *Thames and Hudson Archives.*

99 GEORGE ALEXANDER and Allan Aynesworth in *The Importance of Being Earnest. The Enthoven Collection. By courtesy of the Victoria and Albert Museum, London.*

100 CHARLES HAWTREY (1858–1923) who had also played Lord Goring in the original production of *An Ideal Husband,* played some part in Oscar Wilde's downfall.

101 IRENE VANBRUGH photographed by Alfred Ellis as Gwendolen Fairfax in *The Importance of Being Earnest. Radio Times Hulton Picture Library.*

103 THE EIGHTH MARQUESS OF QUEENSBERRY, John Sholto Douglas (1864–1900), was the cause of Oscar Wilde's tragedy. Phil May (1864–1903), who made this silhouette in 1889, is known principally for his caricatures. From 1895 he was on the staff of *Punch.* He also published a number of collections of comic drawings. *By courtesy of the Trustees of the National Portrait Gallery, London.*

104 OSCAR WILDE, photograph taken in the early 1890s. *Collection the author.*

105 NICE, a photograph showing horse-drawn cabs and buses in the nineties. Wilde had frequently been to the South of France and again just before the trial. *Private collection.*

106 MR JUSTICE HENN COLLINS heard the case of Regina *v.* the Marquess of Queensberry. This caricature by Quiz appeared in the magazine *Vanity Fair* on 14th January 1893.

SIR EDWARD GEORGE CLARKE M.P. (1841–1931) acted as Wilde's leading counsel. When Wilde stood in the dock in his turn, a ruined man, Sir Edward gave his services free. From 1886 to 1892 Clarke was Solicitor-General. He was knighted in 1886. *By courtesy of the Trustees of the National Portrait Gallery.*

107 HOLLOWAY GAOL, built in 1849–51, where Wilde was held while awaiting his first trial. A print dating from about 1865. *Radio Times Hulton Picture Library.*

108 A PREHISTORIC IGUANODON, an illustration in *The Illustrated London News* which was cut out and sent to Wilde anonymously at the time of the trial, with a comment such as 'You Monster' at the bottom. *Radio Times Hulton Picture Library.*

109 MR JUSTICE WILLS heard the second trial of Oscar Wilde and sentenced him to two years' hard labour. Spy's cartoon appeared in the magazine *Vanity Fair,* 25th June 1896.

110 WILDE was sustained during his imprisonment by the hope that his sentence might be shortened. His friends appealed—but with no avail, for the leading writers refused to lend their names. Wilde himself submitted three petitions but they too were unsuccessful. *By courtesy of the Home Office.*

111 FRANS MASEREEL portrays the despair of prison life in these woodcut illustrations to *The Ballad of Reading Gaol,* published in 1924 by Methuen and Company, London.

112 THE MANUSCRIPT of the first and last pages of *De Profundis,* on prison paper; this reproduction is the first ever published, since under the terms of Robert Ross's gift it was not to be accessible until 1960. *By courtesy of the Trustees of the British Museum.*

114 DE PROFUNDIS. The first English edition appeared under Methuen's imprint in March 1905 but was preceded in January and February 1905 by an authorised translation in German by Dr Max Meyerfeld, printed in German characters. The illustration reproduced here is from a German edition in Roman characters, published later that year by S. Fischer Verlag of Berlin, for which Walter Tiemann designed the title-page and initial letters.

115 WILDE'S NUMBER IN READING GAOL was C.3.3 and has been substituted in the frontispiece to *The Ballad of Reading Gaol* for the face of the author. Woodcut by Frans Masereel in the edition of 1924 published by Methuen and Company, London.

117 OSCAR WILDE'S MOTHER in a Daguerreotype. *Collection the author.*

118 ROBERT ROSS (1869–1918) first met Wilde at Oxford in 1886. 'Robbie' was then about seventeen, Wilde thirty-one. Their friendship survived through Wilde's disgrace and ended only with Wilde's death. A portrait by Sir William Rothenstein in about 1890. *In the Collection Sir John Rothenstein and by courtesy of Sir William Rothenstein's executors.*

119 THE HOTEL AT BERNEVAL at which Oscar Wilde stayed after his release. Woodcut by Ethelbert White. *Oscar Wilde, after Reading,* The Beaumont Press, 1921.

Notes

120 THE HOUSE AT BERNEVAL near Dieppe where Wilde settled after his release, using the assumed name of Sebastian Melmoth. *Collection the author.*

121 OSCAR WILDE in front of St Peter's, in the Forum, and on the Capitoline Hill. *Collection the author.*

122 OSCAR WILDE AND LORD ALFRED DOUGLAS soon after Wilde's release. One of several photographs taken at the time. *By courtesy of the Andrew Clark Memorial Library, University of California.*

123, 124 HÔTEL D'ALSACE, rue des Beaux Arts, Paris, where Wilde took rooms in the spring of 1899. Here he died nineteen months later, on 30th November 1900. Rooms 7 and 8 are now called 'The Rooms of Oscar Wilde'. *Photo : Elsa Seedorff.*

125 SIR TRAVERS HUMPHREYS, a photograph taken in 1932. *Photo : Barrett's Photo Press Ltd.*

127 OSCAR WILDE'S TOMB in Père Lachaise; the tombstone is the work of Sir Jacob Epstein. *Photo : Jacqueline Hyde, Paris.*

128 THE MEMORIAL PLAQUE on 16 Tite Street, Chelsea. *Photo : Paterson and Farnill.*

INDEX OF NAMES

Page numbers in italics refer to pictures